"My friend Harry Kraus is an accomplished surgeon and novelist. Now in *Breathing Grace*, he proves himself an insightful spiritual guide, using medical analogies to illustrate great truths. Harry's heart for God and for people spills over on each page."

—**Randy Alcorn**,
author of *Heaven*, *Safely Home*, and *Deception*

"There is no shortage of books on divine grace, but this one is different. Kraus has resorted to a medical metaphor, which he uses especially well in an era when the public is obsessed with health and medicine. But the real lack is spiritual maintenance, which in this presentation is laid out in an interesting and exciting fashion. Thrilling case histories, both medical and spiritual, abound. The human body can go three weeks without food, three days without water, three minutes without oxygen, but spiritual need requires minute by minute dosing, and grace is the remedy. This is not merely a 'how to' book but conveys a simple and satisfying way of life."

—**C. Everett Koop**, M.D.;
former Surgeon General of the United States

"With a physician's skill, my favorite Christian fiction writer dissects the truths of grace with compelling medical analogies. *Breathing Grace* is soul surgery that will transform your life as it probes the core of your relationship with God."

—**David Stevens**, M.D., M.A. (Ethics),
executive director, Christian Medical Society

"*Breathing Grace* by Dr. Harry Kraus, Jr. engages the reader in doing just that, to breathe grace. Dr. Kraus combines creative imagination, professional and clinical perspectives, and cross-cultural insights from his work in Africa with the Scriptures as the word of grace and does so out of his own genuine commitment to Christ. The uniting thread that runs through the book is the emphasis that knowing Jesus in grace makes a radical difference in the way we live and relate to others. Through this work by Kraus the reader will be enriched in spirit and in faith. Our witness as well will be made more effective, for we do not share our faith by an attitude of triumphalism but by an expression of the transforming grace of God as we walk in the Spirit."

—**Myron S. Augsburger**,
former pastor;
former president of Eastern Mennonite University

BREATHING
grace

What You Need
More Than Your Next Breath

Harry Kraus, M.D.

CROSSWAY BOOKS
A PUBLISHING MINISTRY OF
GOOD NEWS PUBLISHERS
WHEATON, ILLINOIS

Library of Congress Cataloging-in-Publication Data
Kraus, Harry Lee, 1960–
    Breathing Grace : what you need more than your next breath / Harry Kraus.
        p.   cm.
    ISBN-13: 978-1-58134-858-3 (hc : alk. paper)
    ISBN 10: 1-58134-858-4
        1. Medicine—Religious aspects—Christianity. 2. Grace (Theology) I. Title.
    BT732.K73 2007
    248.4—dc22   2006029775

For those who have been shepherds in my life, the men who have whispered and shouted grace.

Tom Jones, Dick Dreyer, Bill Oden, Bob Moberg, Dick Blackwell, Billy Powell, Jerry Qualls, Al Lutz, Gerald Martin, Sam Scaggs, Kenton Slabaugh, Vernon Zook, Phil Smuland, and Phil Morrison have all faithfully taught the truths shared in this book, and I am honored to have learned from them.

Table of Contents

Acknowledgments   9

Introduction   11

Part One: The ABC's of Spiritual Resuscitation

Chapter One: Gospel Debt   19

Chapter Two: Making a Diagnosis   25

Chapter Three: Graphing Our Spiritual Vital Signs   35

Chapter Four: **A** is for Airway   41

Chapter Five: **B** is for Breathing   49

Chapter Six: **C** is for Circulation   59

Chapter Seven: Using the ABC's in College   71

Part Two: Problems: What Happens When Respiration Fails

Chapter Eight: Spiritual Emphysema   81

Chapter Nine: Spiritual Anemia: When the Mailmen Go on Strike   91

Chapter Ten: Mouth-to-Mouth Resuscitation: Exhaling Grace   101

Chapter Eleven: Fake Breathing   111

Chapter Twelve: Spiritual Sepsis   123

Chapter Thirteen: Spiritual Emboli   133

Chapter Fourteen: The Great Masquerade   141

Part Three: Treating Gospel Debt

Chapter Fifteen: Defining Oxygen, Defining Grace   153

Chapter Sixteen: The Danger of Noncompliance   163

Notes   169

Scripture Index   171

Acknowledgments

I t is impossible to write about grace and not acknowledge that I have been the recipient of grace from so many human sources. Thus I cannot imagine claiming originality of content when I am breathing out what I've breathed in from others. Through their writings, John Piper, Brennan Manning, Henri Nouwen, C. S. Lewis, Chuck Swindoll, and many others have their fingerprints on my life and therefore on these pages.

Introduction

visited Namanga last weekend. It's a border town straddling Kenya and Tanzania, a place of sweat and heat, a land so thirsty for rain that wild animals die and others misbehave.

A nurse traveling with me pointed to the side of the road. "There's another zebra." The carcass was fresh enough to be identified by the stripes. Soon the vultures would be there, and the evidence would fade. Dust to dust.

A few miles later we saw an ostrich roaming a village within a few meters of the road, pecking at the ground around the small shops in search of food. It doesn't take long to realize that famine changes everything.

Stark contrasts were everywhere. The Muslim Imam sounded the call to prayer, a haunting repetition of Arabic that interrupted my sleep at 4 in the morning. I was restless anyway, lying out on the dusty earth beneath an expansive sky and the thorns of an acacia tree. My sleeping bag was designed for a cooler climate, but it was better to stay protected from mosquitoes carrying malaria, so I opted for sweat and stayed covered up. Several sleepless hours later, with the Muslim call still hanging unabsorbed over the dry earth, another noise interrupted the African night. I crawled from my protected cocoon and stumbled toward the primary school. African Christians were praying. Loudly. Everyone at once. The jumble of voices rose as one vibrant hum, pulsing with perspiration and sincerity.

I visited Namanga as part of a hospital outreach, an effort by which free food and medicine provided the spearhead to carry the gospel into thirsty hearts. During the one-day clinic we saw nearly two thousand people. Maasai tribesmen in traditional dress. Muslim Somali women peering out through small slits in their required head coverings. And all standing out in the searing heat for hours waiting for their chance to see a doctor.

A colleague of mine sat at a worn, wooden desk in a classroom-turned-clinic and looked at the Muslim patient in front of him. "Why do you think we have come?"

The answer came without hesitation. "You want to earn God's favor."

Oh, how wrong the answer, but understandable coming from a graceless religion where the scales weighing good and bad are held in constant focus. I can't imagine sacrificing my job back in America, putting up with mobs of patients, heat, and no running water or electricity in a makeshift clinic to bring the news that you have to earn your way to heaven! Only the fabulous news of free grace could motivate me.

Spiritual famine is unseen by an uninitiated eye, but it is no less prevalent and devastating than the dearth that's been ravaging East Africa. It's not lack of rain but lack of grace that dries the soul and makes us dull to the water-whispers of God's Spirit.

But God's grace is amazing, abundant, free, and available. *So why is spiritual famine an epidemic both inside and outside the church?*

Because although we've come to Christ by recognizing grace, few of us have carried it along as essential equipment on the Christian path. We give mental assent to the truth of the gospel message, but we live our lives in famine, as if we could earn God's favor. We are God's children, but our souls are dry.

My life would be complete if only I could have peace of mind.

If only my boss would recognize my contributions.

If only my coworkers weren't such jerks.

If only my spouse was different.

If only I could get a divorce.

If only my children would behave.

If only my mother and father wouldn't fight.

If only my pastor wouldn't keep asking for money.

If only the investments would pay off, or my portfolio was fatter, or my house was bigger, or I had a new car. If only I could just get ahead.

If only I could stop lusting. This will be the last time I look at this Internet site . . .

Of course I'm depressed. You would be too if you'd been hurt like I have.

In truth, our frustration, anxiety, and lack of fulfillment and victory over sin have more to do with our reaction to circumstances than with the circumstances themselves, and in turn our reactions are governed by our understanding of God's grace. God never promised a pain-free life, but he did promise that his grace is *all we need* in our search for peace and fulfillment.

> "My grace is sufficient for you, for my power is made perfect in weakness."
>
> —2 Corinthians 12:9

For many, *grace* is just a word we sing, a recitation of mindless words on a Sunday morning. We carry on with life, unmoved and unmotivated by the magnitude of God's character. Others have given up completely, having heard the word but failing to understand its depth.

Grace. An athletic quality, right?
Grace. Aren't we supposed to call royalty, "Your Grace?"
Sure I know about grace. I say grace before meals, at least when I'm not in a restaurant. [1]

God's grace? His kindness, right? For too many *grace* is an out-there word, too abstract to curl into your arms and embrace. The enormity of its importance has been lost in contemporary language. It seems a bit like the quality of niceness exuded by Mr. Rogers on his beloved TV show. Our concept is anemic, weakened by a society content with substitutes, false gospels of self-worship, and materialism.

But God's grace is amazing. I almost hesitate to use that adjective, for fear you will skip over its meaning. Amazing. Astonishing. Astounding. My Microsoft dictionary defines *amazing* this way: "So extraordinary or wonderful as to be barely believable or cause extreme surprise."

So yes, amazing is a perfectly good description of the gospel of grace. The Bible says it this way:

> You are not under law but under grace.
> —Romans 6:14

> . . . so that in the coming ages he might show the immeasurable riches of his grace.
> —Ephesians 2:7

> But grow in the grace and knowledge of our Lord and Savior Jesus Christ.
> —2 Peter 3:18

> . . . serve one another, as good stewards of God's varied grace.
> —1 Peter 4:10

> Through him we have also obtained access by faith into
> this grace in which we stand.
>
> —Romans 5:2

We are "under" grace, we "stand" in grace, we "grow" in grace, and we are "stewards" of grace. God's grace has "immeasurable riches." Yes, this grace is much bigger than the niceness exuded by Mr. Rogers and his neighborhood.

Grace notes are small embellishments at the edge of a melody.[2] For too many of us, our understanding of grace has been like that: something at the periphery of our experience, nice perhaps, ornamental, but nothing substantial. This book is all about moving our concept of the gospel from grace notes to the major chord of our lives, something that undergirds the melody every day, every hour. This book is about moving our understanding of grace from one of God's minor attributes to the central feature of his posture toward his children, the quality that governs his every action toward us on the road of redemption.

OK, grace sounds good, but what is it exactly? Grace is like mercy, right?

No. Grace and mercy flow from the same stream of God's character, but they have distinct differences. Perhaps you've heard the common explanations: Grace is getting what I don't deserve—that is, heaven and every blessing on this side of glory. Mercy is not getting what I do deserve—that is, hell and eternal separation from God.

Those definitions are workable, but I'd like to offer my own definition of grace that I'll expand on later.

Grace is a godly characteristic that determines God's posture toward his children whereby he generously and freely loves, forgives, favors, and exalts undeserving sinners into sonship.

Earmark this page so you can find the definition quickly. In our journey together we'll look at the inflow and outflow of grace, how it functions and how it can be obstructed. In the end we'll return to this starting point and push out the definition even further.

I'm a surgeon, and after a day's work my wife often comments, "You smell like the hospital." It's not an unpleasant thing, just a clinical fragrance from scrubbing my hands with antiseptic soaps.

Likewise, this book carries a clinical aroma because naturally I've wrapped the concept of grace in a medical metaphor. We need a moment-by-moment supply of oxygen for physical survival, and we need a moment-by-moment supply of grace for soul survival.

Some of us have endured dry, graceless Christian lives that have wearied us, sickened us, and tempted us to surrender. *If this is all there is, what good is Christianity?*

Read on, tired traveler. Famine of soul should prompt us to look for deeper streams of grace. We need a signpost pointing to a life lived in appropriate grace saturation. We've heard reports of a promised land of milk and honey, but we seem to dwell in a land where we're thirsty for more. We need a spiritual resuscitation. So that's where we'll begin.

For Further Reflection

1. Does the Muslim patient's response—"You want to earn God's favor"—at all describe why you do what you do, whether at home, at work, or even at church? Why or why not?

2. Do you agree that "although we've come to Christ by recognizing grace, few of us have carried it along as essential equipment on the Christian path"? Why would this be so?

3. Have you personally found God's promise to the apostle Paul ("My grace is sufficient for you, for my power is made perfect in weakness") to be true? Explain.

4. Of the Scripture passages on grace shared in this Introduction, which means the most to you, and why?

5. Is God's grace a major chord or merely grace notes in your life? Why do you think this is so?

PART ONE

The ABC's of Spiritual Resuscitation

CHAPTER ONE

Gospel Debt

Few events sear themselves on the memory of a surgeon with more heat than a patient without an airway.

Seconds tick away, each a hammer blow against survival. A cascade of negative metabolic consequences rockets forward with the imminent precipice of death in sharp focus.

Without a workable immediate plan, the patient will free-fall into eternity.

I'll never forget Ray Stafford. I was chief resident on the trauma service the night Ray died on my watch.

My trauma-alert pager sounded the five-minute warning to assemble the team. The Sikorsky medical transport helicopter raced toward the university hospital rooftop carrying a critical patient. I stopped in the small cubicle that housed the flight dispatch in the center of the emergency room. "Hi, Joe, what's coming?"

He leaned back in his chair and gave me a bullet presentation. "Twenty-seven-year-old male, victim of a close-range GSW to the face." GSW is traumaese for gunshot wound.

I smiled in spite of my fatigue. A penetrating trauma like this one meant surgery, a welcome contrast to the majority of blunt-trauma victims whom general surgeons baby-sit for the orthopedic service. "Sweet," I said. It's a response I doubt non-surgeons will understand. I wasn't glad the patient was injured, but if it was going to happen, I wanted it to happen when I could gain experience through the case. That's the twisted sort of attitude that makes a competent surgeon.

A few minutes later I met Ray as the team transferred him off the transport stretcher onto one of ours in a trauma bay.

I observed the rise of his chest and placed my stethoscope against his thorax. *Airway. Breathing. Circulation.* "What happened to you?"

His face contorted with pain. "Some dude shot me," he grunted.

I'd heard a similar story dozens of times. It was always "some dude." Later I learned that a vengeful father shot Ray because of Ray's intimate relationship with the angry man's daughter. The interesting stories always came out later, but in the midst of the initial workup the histories all sounded the same and were surgically succinct: "young white male involved in a social altercation sustaining a GSW to the . . ."

Ray had a small entrance wound on his left cheek. His right upper neck was swollen, and an exit wound was visible on the right lateral, posterior neck near the hairline.

The team swarmed. Vital signs were assessed. Blood pressure was 140 systolic. A nurse secured a second intravenous line. *Follow the ABC's.* A chest X-ray was taken. A urinary catheter was inserted. After a phone consultation with my surgical attending, Ray was taken to the angio suite for an arteriogram, a specialized X-ray that visualizes the blood vessels and provides a road map to locate possible arterial injury.

I threw the X-rays up on the view-box as they came out of the processor. I examined the films, still warm from the developing process. An arterial blush clouded the area lateral to the internal carotid artery, an indication of bleeding, a serious injury that was partially contained, a situation that needed stat attention before the artery free-ruptured, ensuring exsanguination and death. Although stable for the moment, the patient needed emergency surgery and was soon whisked across the hall to the operating suite while I called in my attending surgeon.

Blood made the neck bulge, tenting up the skin near the exit wound. How long would it be before the bleeding could not be contained or the airway was compressed by the expanding collection of blood?

Nurses positioned Ray on the operating table as his eyes widened in fear. The anesthesiologist prepared to put the patient to sleep and slid a breathing tube into Ray's trachea. The vascular surgeons scrubbed their hands.

But the patient's restlessness escalated, his knuckles whitening as he gripped the sides of the operating table. And then without warning he wretched, vomiting what appeared to be undiluted blood. *A lot of blood.*

Ray sat bolt upright, fighting for air. Then he fell back, thudding against the operating table. Pulseless. Without respiratory effort. *Time for the ABC's.*

The anesthesiologist slid a laryngoscope into Ray's mouth. "I can't see anything," he yelled. "There's too much blood."

With the airway obstructed, without oxygen, Ray was dying in front of me. On my watch.

Oxygen debt: When our bodies are screaming for payment and the currency is oxygen.

At that moment my patient was in shock, a clinical diagnosis defined as inadequate flow to the end organs, kidneys, heart, and brain. The vital organs are starving for oxygen, and what defines the crisis is a lack of the same.

At a cellular level, all the metabolic activity is screaming for payment, and the currency is oxygen. Without an adequate supply, a situation occurs that we know as *oxygen debt.*

We've all experienced this at some time or other, perhaps at the end of a footrace across the school playground. Our heart races, and our respirations increase, all in an attempt to supply oxygen to starving muscles. We collapse with our hands on our knees. All other activity ceases as we gasp to overcome the debt of oxygen.

So what does all this have to do with the gospel?

Gospel debt: When our souls are demanding payment and the currency is grace.

Sometimes subtle and insidious, but no less critical, is the current epidemic found within the church and within all of us: gospel debt.

Just as every cell (one hundred trillion in one human body!) requires a constant supply of oxygen, so every spiritual, emotional, and social aspect of our lives need a constant saturation with the gospel of grace.

Surgeons are trained to think on their feet, to make life-and-death decisions in spite of their own fatigue. Dozens of other details clamor for the surgeon's attention, distracting from the priorities at hand. Fortunately, there are simple guidelines, a mnemonic to focus the priorities. *Airway. Breathing. Circulation.* Simple enough to be remembered by everyone. Succinct. To the point. The surgeon targets the critical first need, the life-or-death problem that will determine the patient's ultimate end.

Without oxygen a death spiral begins. The metabolic machinery within every cell unravels into inefficiency. Unless reversed, irreversible consequences loom as the brain cells starve and die.

Without the true gospel, we quickly turn to other methods to fill the void—false gospels of self-sufficiency, blaming circumstances or others—all futile attempts to make up for a *gospel debt*. Without the gospel, we begin a death spiral of sorts, a slide into a life empty of peace. Joyless. Mechanical. We follow the rules. Outwardly holy, inwardly starving.

But just as the trauma surgeon turns to the ABC's, we can turn to the ABC's of spiritual resuscitation. Guidelines simple enough to be remembered by us all, even in the clamor of life's everyday disasters. So that's where we will start. The beginning, the elementary school chalkboard of our Christian lives. We're going back to the ABC's . . .

But what about Ray? We left our story as he fell lifeless onto the operating table. At that point a branch of his carotid artery had ruptured into the back of his throat. Ray was in full circulatory collapse, his airway obscured by blood and the swelling from the bullet's path.

So I followed the ABC's.

I made an incision through the skin, palpating for landmarks, opened the cricothyroid membrane, and inserted a breathing tube directly into the trachea, actions taken to secure an *Airway*. We began to ventilate through the tube, forcing oxygen into his lungs. That took care of *Breathing*. CPR was initiated, externally pumping on Ray's chest as additional blood and fluids were pushed into his empty veins, actions taken to support *Circulation* until a pulse was detected again.

The ABC's guided our steps. And Ray was brought back to life.

Of course, that didn't solve all of Ray's other problems. An angry father still preferred to see Ray pulseless and cold rather than carousing with the madman's daughter. So we admitted our patient under an assumed name to protect him from the father who wanted him dead. And in a few days we let Ray go again, with a scar on his neck as a permanent reminder of his brush with the Grim Reaper. So we cared for his physical life, following established guidelines. What he needed next was someone to guide him through a spiritual resuscitation to reorder his dysfunctional life.

But we're all like Ray. We may not have the same set of problems, but we're all dysfunctional in our own ways. One moment we're saturated with the gospel, content in the sufficiency of the cross. The next, we're in gospel debt, showing all the symptoms. Some are subtle, visible only after dissection below the surface of false gospels. Some are pulse-pounding terrifying and require urgent intervention. That's when we need a solution, the ABC's.

It takes a scalpel to dissect below the skin.

It takes a spiritual scalpel of sorts to dissect beneath the scab of self-reliance. But I'm rushing ahead. Before we can offer a solution, we need to make a proper diagnosis.

For Further Reflection

1. What is gospel debt? How do you see this in your own life?

2. How does gospel debt relate to divine grace?

3. Do you really need grace as constantly as you need oxygen? Why?

4. Do you agree that "Without the true gospel, we quickly turn to other methods to fill the void—false gospels of self-sufficiency"? How does this reveal itself in your life? When you see this, what should you do?

5. "Without the gospel, we . . . follow the rules [but are] outwardly holy, inwardly starving." How can you be starving if you're following God's rules, if you're "outwardly holy"?

CHAPTER TWO

Making a Diagnosis

For the medical student, surgical attending rounds are simultaneously delightful and agonizing. Students bask in an approving nod from the chief and wince under his critical gaze.

The surgeon moved down a spacious hallway with his entourage around him—three med students, two interns, a junior resident, and a chief resident. Room to room, patient to patient they trekked, using the Socratic method of questioning, with a probing for deficiencies and the dispensing of gray-haired wisdom in progress.

The attending surgeon's white coat was knee-length, crisply starched, and stain-free. The med student's was short, bulging with memory aids, wrinkled from a twenty-minute nap on an ER stretcher, and stained with vending machine coffee.

The attending, Dr. Arensen, gazed through his bifocals and called the medical student "doctor" even though a degree was months away. "Dr. Smith, you are called to see a fourteen-year-old female with right lower quadrant pain. What do you do?"

"Intravenous antibiotics and appendectomy."

The attending surgeon didn't smile. He shook his head slowly. The student was eager but too green for clinical efficiency or patient safety. "How about talking to your patient, young doctor? History first," he said, holding up a finger, "physical exam next."

Too often the inexperienced student rushes to treatment or expensive diagnostic maneuvers such as CT scans instead of careful history-taking and a physical examination.

A surgeon wouldn't take a patient to the operating room without a diagnosis, or at least a strong indication that a surgical problem existed. And we mustn't rush to the treatment of ABC's for gospel debt before understanding the signs and symptoms that lead us to the diagnosis.

Remember Ray? Oxygen debt can have symptoms and signs that are subtle:

The patient's restlessness escalated, his knuckles whitening as he gripped the sides of the operating table.

Or in-your-face obvious:

Ray sat bolt upright, fighting for air. Then he fell back, thudding against the operating table. Pulseless. Without respiratory effort.

I've divided my surgical professional life between North America and Africa. The contrasts abound, but one distinct advantage for the physician in a developing country is the assurance that the temptation to skip to tests and treatments is minimal. When you don't have a CT scanner, you have to talk to your patient. You have to look for subtle clues to make the right diagnosis.

It's no different when we think about gospel debt. How can we apply a solution if we don't realize there's a problem?

A thorough medical history involves probing into every area, a point-by-point questioning of possible problems involving every organ system. And so to make a diagnosis of gospel debt, we begin to ask questions.

Taking a review of systems: Now you've stopped preachin' and started meddlin'!

Are you experiencing restlessness, a sense that true joy or peace lies just around the next bend? *There has to be more to life than this.*

Are you critical of yourself? Your children? Your spouse? *Don't you dare act that way in church!*

Do you have a sense that you are never quite good enough or never able to do enough? Are you anxious in service, overwrought with good activities? Is business for God crowding out communion with him?

Are you irritated by others' lack of respect for your thoughts, your suggestions, or your time? When others interrupt your speech, are you able to respond with grace, or do you find yourself raising your voice in an attempt to be heard?

Are you consumed with outward appearances? The latest fashion? Feel anxious if you miss your time at the gym or if your scales reveal a few extra pounds? *I'm sure I'd be happy if I just lost that "winter-twenty" I gained.*

What about satisfaction? Are you always thinking about the next car, the next piece of furniture, the next house, the next vacation? Do you make one purchase only to lose interest and find yourself turning to a new computer, new toy, or new technology that's always faster and better, with more bells and whistles for your friends to admire? *I need a wide-screen TV to attract the youth group to my house.*

Are you irritated when you seem to be the only one teaching Sunday school or serving on church committees year after year? Or when everyone and their brother ask you for support for their summer mission trip to Mexico? *I can't remember ever talking to this guy until he asked for money.*

Are you angry over the loss of a spouse, a failed marriage, or a rebellious child?

Do you lose yourself in entertainment, food, video games, fiction, sports, or pharmaceuticals and/or alcohol in an attempt to patch over bitterness, boredom, or a lack of peace or satisfaction? *I work hard. I deserve to relax. What's wrong with that?*

Are you able to give without telling anyone, to do service without a pat on the back or applause, even when it's clearly deserved? *I need to tell others what I gave in order to inspire them to give, to set the example.*

Do you feel guilty? Anxious? *I'll never forget the time I . . .*

Have you lost the sheer wonder of God's holiness or the joy of having your sins washed away? *I'm not really that bad.*

Have impatience and irritability replaced compassion? Has a demand for perfection replaced gentleness? *Why is that family always late for church?* Or, *I can't take the flaky way Lucy always says "Lord" every other sentence when she's praying.*

Do you think more of your retirement plan and your investment diversification than you do of a strategy to fulfill the Great Commission? *If I invest now, I'll be able to give more later.*

Do you justify your wandering eyes? *It's OK if I admire the menu as long as I eat at home.* Or, *It's just a Sports Illustrated. I didn't buy it to look at the swimsuit beauties.* How about Internet pornography? *I'm not hurting anyone.*

Are you casually indifferent to sin? Have you stopped calling sin sin? *The movie I watched last night wasn't that bad. Sure, it had a little language and a few adult situations, but that's just real life.*

Has concern for offending another's false religious beliefs overtaken your love for the lost? Has political correctness taken priority over obedience?

Do you make excuses, excuses, excuses?

I'm steppin' on my own shoes here. I'm asking the questions, but we're all made of the same stuff.

If I've learned one thing in the last thirty years (yes, I'm a lot older than thirty, but that seemed like a good time span to me), it's that my ability to deceive myself is a natural talent. In all of these areas it is so easy to wear self-righteous glasses that allow me to see dust in your eyes but not the log in my own.

The point of the questions is not to focus on how bad we are, although we're much worse than we think! The point is not to concentrate on these problems but to see them as symptoms of the endemic pathology they represent, the pathology present in all of us: *gospel debt.*

All of the things I've listed above stem in some way from our reliance on false gospels that we invent to make up for gospel debt. If we're going to understand when we're low on the gospel, we need to first look at what the gospel is and means.

But, you say, I've heard the gospel message, I've been to the altar. I've given my life to Christ. I've believed the gospel, but I still have all of these problems you mentioned!

Exactly.

But the gospel is bigger than the message you believed the day you first realized your need for a Savior. It's a lot bigger than "asking Jesus into your heart," the elementary phrase that sums up the theological depth of many of our pew-sitters.

The gospel is simple. And huge. God the Father showed us his grace not by overlooking our sin but by demanding a payment. That payment, enacted at one time for all our sins—past, present, and future—placed us in right standing before a holy God. Now we are able and deserve to enjoy all of the benefits of sonship. The penalty for our misdeeds was fully paid by the sacrifice of Jesus Christ and affected the great switch: our sin for his righteousness. The record of our sins for the record of his accomplishments. It's an unfair deal from the start, but one that takes away my breath and thickens my voice whenever I start to remember all that he did.

What did I contribute to my salvation? Nothing but my need.

According to the gospel, what did I contribute to my salvation? Nothing but my need. I didn't deserve it, couldn't work for it, and can't change God's mind about it. I love the words of the old hymn:

All the fitness he requireth is to feel your need of him.[3]

What did God contribute to my salvation? Everything.

What is God's part? Everything. He alone can call me, awaken my desire, help me see my need, and pay the price. He never doubts the adequacy of his salvation or sees me outside the righteousness that now surrounds and defines me (Jesus' righteousness is now mine!).

So how does all this relate to gospel debt, to all the symptoms we listed and the million we didn't? Simply put, the blessings of the gospel extend far beyond the fire escape benefit. Not only do we get out of what we deserve—hell—but we are let in on the blessings of sonship.

In subsequent chapters we'll look closely at the ABC's of getting out of gospel debt. But we needed to start with a correct diagnosis, a general understanding of what the disease looks like. And to understand what it is to live without it, we've looked at what the gospel is.

Don't try this at home.

Oxygen debt is easier to diagnose in Caucasians than in people "of color," especially some African tribes. You see, hemoglobin, the molecule that carries the oxygen to our cells, absorbs light at a different frequency when it is carrying all the oxygen it can handle (we call this hemoglobin saturated) than when it is carrying less oxygen (lower in saturation). That's why arterial blood (with saturated hemoglobin) is bright red, and venous blood (more desaturated) is deep purple. And that's why if you place a transparent plastic bag over your Caucasian friend's head, and cinch it tightly around the neck, he or she will begin to change. The lips will darken, then take on a bluish hue almost like that blue hair tint that grandmas use to make their gray hair shine. The skin pales, then turns violet as oxygen is taken from the cells and is emptied from the blood.

Gospel debt comes from an inadequate gospel saturation, and the symptoms are more obvious in some of us than in others. Some of us may be spiritual Africans, able to hide our symptoms of gospel debt. Here I mean no slam on my African brothers and sisters—I am only extending my oxygen debt metaphor as an example. Sometimes from the outside everything looks fine. The good works are in place. But inside we all suffer the malady, and we all need to refocus on the ABC's.

I don't really want to close this chapter on a negative note, with the heaviness of gospel debt symptoms fresh in your mind. Instead think again about how rich a salvation God has given. Meditate on these verses that remind us of the depth of this gospel of grace. In future chapters we'll look at the solution, the way out of gospel debt.

> But now that you have been set free from sin and have become slaves of God, the fruit you get leads to sanctification and its end, eternal life. For the wages of sin is death, but the free gift of God is eternal life in Christ Jesus our Lord.
>
> —Romans 6:22-23

> And my God will supply every need of yours according to his riches in glory in Christ Jesus.
>
> —Philippians 4:19

> Blessed be the God and Father of our Lord Jesus Christ,
> who has blessed us in Christ with every spiritual blessing
> in the heavenly places, even as he chose us in him before
> the foundation of the world, that we should be holy and
> blameless before him.
>
> —Ephesians 1:3-4

> . . . so that in Christ Jesus the blessing of Abraham might
> come to the Gentiles, so that we might receive the prom-
> ised Spirit through faith.
>
> —Galatians 3:14

> Therefore, since we have been justified by faith, we have
> peace with God through our Lord Jesus Christ. Through
> him we have also obtained access by faith into this grace
> in which we stand, and we rejoice in hope of the glory
> of God.
>
> —Romans 5:1-2

> There is therefore now no condemnation for those who
> are in Christ Jesus.
>
> —Romans 8:1

One more verse for now. I love this phrase:

> . . . the unsearchable riches of Christ . . .
>
> —Ephesians 3:8

Some of us have seen ourselves as we read through the list of questions in our spiritual history. We read what the Bible promises: every
spiritual blessing, every need met, no condemnation, peace, unsearch-
able riches. *So why the disconnect between what I read and what I
experience?*

Remember our medical student, eager but green? I feel the tension to rush ahead to treatment, but we haven't done a thorough

examination yet. Let's not forget the sage advice from the clinician with gray hair.

"History first," he said, holding up a finger, *"physical exam next."*

For Further Reflection

1. Do you ever think, *There must be more to life than this*? Why? What should you do with such troubling thoughts?

2. Do you agree that "the gospel is bigger than the message you believed the day you first realized your need for a Savior. It's a lot bigger than 'asking Jesus into your heart'"? Explain.

3. Do you agree that you contributed nothing at all to your salvation? Isn't this an insult to you? Why or why not?

4. Why is your gospel debt not always obvious, and sometimes hard to detect?

5. Of the Scripture passages on our great salvation quoted toward the end of the chapter, which means the most to you, and why?

CHAPTER THREE

Graphing Our Spiritual Vital Signs

The patient is given a paper gown and is told to take off his clothes. "Have a seat on the table. The doctor will be right in."

Right. I've heard that line before.

So you sit, cold, a bit irritated, hoping you will be able to pick up the kids from school on time.

I don't know anyone who likes getting a physical exam, especially involving the intimate parts. And it's not just the patients who are uncomfortable. Just ask medical students who are sent into a hospital ward with their new leather bag of instruments. They fumble through the history, the detailed review of systems, and a complete physical. To finish it off, they rush through the rectal exam, hoping the patient won't ask what they found. Chances are they were a bit too self-conscious to take the time to feel anything except their own discomfort.

I remember my first history and physical. It was at the old Veterans Administration Hospital in Richmond, Virginia. They unleashed the second-year medical students into a ward with only a thin curtain to draw around patients for privacy. So not only did our patients get to hear our questions—twenty other patients did too. All around, I'd say it was a pretty entertaining hour (actually my first one took an hour and a half!) for the ward.

Now a pet peeve of mine is seeing an inadequate physical exam record, especially omissions just because a doctor was in a hurry or uncomfortable. If I read, "deferred" next to the rectal or pelvic exam of an intern history and physical report, I'm likely to ask him to go back and correct his deficiency.

I remember a crusty, retired army officer who came to see me about his hernia. He was mildly irritated that I performed a complete exam, but thankful that I found his rectal cancer.

The exam begins with the vital signs: temperature, respiratory rate, heart rate, blood pressure. In the hospital these values are often graphed to highlight the recognition of a trend. If you've taken your child to a pediatrician, the charts and graphs are sure to come out. Anxious mothers peer over the doctor's shoulder to see how their child stacks up against the norms. For the longest time I knew exactly what percentile my boys were in regard to head circumference, height, and weight. Every parent is happy if his or her child is in the middle of the graph.

Why the charts and graphs? Because more important than any isolated value is how that value is changing with time.

A trend in the vital signs is always more important than an isolated value.

A surgeon approaches the foot of a patient's bed in the ICU. The modern setup has the aura of our techno age as monitors flash numbers in an eerie green. The patient lies beneath a tangle of wires connecting him to machines measuring oxygen saturation, cardiac activity, and blood pressure. Tubes empty fluid from the stomach and the urinary bladder into bags that hang on the edge of the bed. Dr. Alice Newberry picks up the bedside chart and listens as the intern begins a presentation.

"Mr. Stevens is a sixty-two-year-old male who is six days status post a sigmoid colon resection for a perforated diverticulum. His T-max was 102 degrees Fahrenheit."

Dr. Newberry frowns. "He has an intraabdominal abscess."

The intern is puzzled. How does the attending know what's going on inside the patient's abdomen without further investigation?

Because she is looking at the temperature graph. When the dots were connected, it looked like a picket fence, with nightly spikes of fever, an indication of a collection of infection in the abdomen. An expensive CT scan will confirm the diagnosis, but the first clue was a graph of the temperature.

Another scenario plays out in sub-Sahara Africa almost every day. The doctor is rounding on a men's ward, twenty beds in one big room, close enough that if you wanted to walk from one end to the other without touching the floor, you could do it, walking from bed to bed without a big jump. He looks at the graph of the temperature. A fever occurred last night and three days before. The doctor orders treatment for malaria. In many resource-poor hospitals, the medicine is cheaper than further investigation. In Kenya, AIDS is the number one killer, malaria the second. Any fever, especially one occurring every few days with no other obvious cause, is malaria.

So the vital signs are the first thing and, when trended, give invaluable information to the treating physicians and nurses.

What if we could graph our spiritual vital signs?

If Doctor Jesus took a look at our lives, what would he see? Would he pick up our bedside chart and smile? Or would he frown and order treatment for gospel debt?

After we become Christians, our appreciation of God's holiness generally increases. In addition, as we travel farther down the road of Christian maturity, we understand more and more of our own sinfulness. Before we come to Christ (an event that required the ABC's, which I promise I'll get to soon!), we appreciate neither our sinfulness nor God's righteousness. At the time of our salvation, what we understand about the gospel perfectly bridges the gap between our sin and God's holiness. At that point in time, we see the sacrifice of Christ as completely sufficient to pay the penalty for our sin and place us in right standing with our Holy Father, providing access into all the benefits of sonship. As we grow in our Christian faith, our knowledge of our own sin and God's holiness increases. As long as our understanding of the gospel grows, no problem.

But . . .

This is real life, so there's always a *but*, isn't there?

When our understanding of the adequacy of the gospel doesn't keep pace with our appreciation for God's holiness or our own need, gospel debt results. If we could graph gospel debt, it would look like this: Imagine one line increasing from left to right with time, representing our understanding of God's holiness. A second line, sinking away from the first, descends across the page, representing our increasing appreciation of our own depravity. Draw a cross between the two divergent lines so that the top and bottom of the cross just touch the two lines. With the cross in that position, it fully fills the gap between our depravity and God's holiness. If, however, our vision of the cross (in effect, the size of the cross in our imagined diagram) doesn't keep pace with our understanding of God's holiness or our own depravity, the size of the cross isn't large enough to fill the gap. Any space between the top of the cross and the line representing God's holiness or any space between the bottom of the cross and the line representing our own depravity represents gospel debt. Whenever we resort to false gospels to make up the gap, we're acting out of a gospel debt.[4]

False gospels? What am I talking about? Anything we do to try to make up the gap. Remember what the gap is made of: the vast difference between our purity and God's. The point isn't that the gap hasn't been perfectly bridged by the cross. It's that experientially our perception of Christ's sacrifice doesn't continue to bridge the gap.

How do I try to bridge the gap? I can resort to two tactics. Either I try to downplay my own sinfulness, or I make myself look better than I really am.

The self-deceit is subtle. We slip into gospel debt almost as easily as we breathe. One minute we're serving Christ out of proper motive (a love for him or for the lost); the next, we're seeking the admiration of men. This is the essence of pride, a false gospel seen on our imagined diagram above the inadequate cross.

And our ability to downplay our own sinfulness is just as prevalent. Even the child-molester-murderer on Death Row plays this little mind game in an attempt to justify himself. *At least I admit I'm bad. Those Christian hypocrites don't even see their problems.* This is the gospel debt represented on our imagined diagram as the area below the inadequate cross, between the bottom of the cross and a line representing our depravity.

We slip into gospel debt almost as naturally as breathing. Perhaps that's why our need for oxygen is the perfect metaphor to illustrate our need of the gospel. Every day. Every second!

The reality of God's provision in the cross is that it dwarfs the chasm between our sin and God's righteousness. When we are living in gospel debt, it's not because the cross is inadequate. It is because our perception or experience of the cross is inadequate. Unfortunately, most of the church lives out most of its life experiencing grace debt. In truth, we can't live a life completely free of gospel debt all the time. But . . .

(Don't you love it when a *but* is finally positive?)

. . . don't be discouraged. Remember what I said about a vital sign trend being more important than a single value? Well, that's true for our spiritual lives as well. We mess up. We're human. But don't despair. The trend is what is important. And that's what this book is all about: diagnosing and treating gospel debt, so that our spiritual vital sign chart will reflect more and more time recognizing the adequacy of God's grace and less and less time wallowing in gospel debt.

And that's where we're headed with the ABC's.

For Further Reflection

1. "A trend in the vital signs is always more important than an isolated value." Why is this significant regarding your spiritual life?

2. Can you graph your spiritual vital signs? Do you want to? Why or why not?

3. Was the diagram that was described helpful? In what ways? What is the basic message of that diagram?

4. "When our understanding of the adequacy of the gospel doesn't keep pace with our appreciation for God's holiness or our own need, gospel debt results." What does this mean? How can you apply this to your own life?

5. To what false gospels do you most easily fall prey? Why? How can you keep from being seduced by them?

CHAPTER FOUR

A Is for Airway

ook both ways before you cross the street."

"Don't ever get in a car with a stranger."

Good advice given over and over from loving mothers. But some messages are so obvious that caring mothers don't need to speak them at all.

"Never bite a rattlesnake."

Sounds crazy. And it was. But Billy Dean's frontal lobes had been generously lubricated with beer, so he wasn't behaving rationally that day.

And yes, this is true. Billy Dean was a real patient, treated by my surgical practice in Virginia.

And yes, names are changed to protect the innocent, or in this case the not so innocent. Perhaps *innocent* isn't the right word. Stupid comes to mind, but that isn't against the law.

Billy Dean enjoyed the low rumble of his Harley-Davidson but decided he'd had too many beers to use it that day. So down the country road on his bicycle he wobbled, the perfect activity on a warm summer afternoon. But that pesky rattlesnake changed everything. It was just lying in the road absorbing the heat when Billy decided to have a little fun.

After all, how hard can it be to catch a rattlesnake? That Australian crocodile-hunter chap on TV made it look easy.

So Billy dismounted his bicycle and soon had a snake by the tail. But controlling the other end of the snake presented a problem. The tail held those neat rattles, but the head contained another surprise.

Fangs. Venom.

And a moment later the snake took revenge on Billy's hand.

And that made Billy Dean mad. And beer made Billy stupid.

So, believing in eye-for-an-eye, tooth-for-a-tooth judgment, Billy decided to bite back. Now by this time Billy had the snake firmly gripped behind its head. So when he lifted it to his mouth to execute his attack plan, the snake bit him again, this time sinking its fangs in Billy's cheek, right at the corner of his mouth.

Fast-forward an hour. Billy Dean arrives in the local emergency room, carried in by rescue personnel who are destined to repeat Billy's story a thousand times.

By the time he came to the hospital, Billy was showing signs of a significant venom effect. He would need antivenom *immediately*, but that wasn't priority number one. Priority number one is always the same: *A* is for Airway.

Breathing had become difficult for Billy as the swelling around his voice box and vocal cords increased. We use the word *stridor* to describe the whistling noise that is made when the airway is closing off.

Stridor isn't a happy, willful whistle like you make when you close your lips around a song. Stridor is scary stuff to the emergency physician. It means the airway is being lost and action must be taken to save the patient *NOW!*

Fortunately for Billy, the physician staffing the emergency room was able to insert a breathing tube through his swelling vocal cords and preserve a passage to allow oxygen back into Billy's starving body.

Have you ever noticed that when breath is mentioned in the Bible, it is often coupled with the word *life*? For example:

> Then the LORD God formed the man of dust from the ground and breathed into his nostrils the *breath of life.*
>
> —Genesis 2:7, emphasis added

It goes without saying that without a way in, the oxygen available all around us does little to help. Without a way to let the oxygen in, Billy Dean was a goner. And not within a day or two. No oxygen, no life. Within minutes. It's that simple. And it's that important.

Let's look again at the problem of gospel debt. Is there a spiritual equivalent to airway obstruction, a sure way to choke off the life-giving grace that our souls need for resuscitation? Sure. Here we encounter the first initial in our treatment plan.

A is for acknowledge your need.

That's it? Acknowledge your need?

Absolutely.

Remember what we contributed to our salvation? Nothing but our need. We came to Christ at a point when the lights came on and our sin was finally exposed. And all we had to do was realize it. This is the essence of repentance. No one ever comes to Christ for salvation who doesn't see his or her own problem. And people never find themselves free from the entanglement of gospel debt if they don't realize their own need.

This is why pride sounds the death knell for our spiritual lives. It completely shuts off the airway, the avenue for God's abundant grace to flow into our needy souls. When we operate out of the false gospel of pride, we are blind to our sin, blind to our need, and blind to the available solution.

The Holy Spirit operates like a gentleman. He doesn't force his way in. The problem is self-evident: we don't ask for help when we are self-sufficient. And this is the great irony and tragedy of being human. We seem wired to desire control. I should know. Surgeons are all too typical in this regard! And when we are in the driver's seat, the Holy Spirit slips quietly into the back. But what fool would insist that Jeff Gordon sit in the back while we compete in a NASCAR race with us behind the wheel? But that pales as an effective metaphor. Perhaps the one Jeremiah used is more appropriate:

> For my people have committed two evils: they have forsaken me, the fountain of living waters, and hewed out cisterns for themselves, broken cisterns that can hold no water.
>
> —Jeremiah 2:13

John Piper has explained sin as what we do when we are not satisfied with God.[5] We fall when we believe a false gospel, a lie that proclaims that satisfaction can be found outside of Christ and the treasure that he is. And so in our blind pride we turn away from the Niagara flow of God's love and grace, and we wallow instead in the small water source we have built for ourselves. We are children content to splash in mud puddles when a fountain is available. But we don't see the source of grace because the airway is obstructed. Grace won't flow in where pride obstructs.

The Bible drives this message home over and over. I think the repetition is for people like me. Why is it so hard to admit we are wrong? Why is concealing our need (sin) so much easier than bringing it into the open? Hear these words from the Bible.

> Whoever conceals his transgressions will not prosper, but he who confesses and forsakes them will obtain mercy.
>
> —Proverbs 28:13

> But he gives more grace. Therefore it says, "God opposes the proud, but gives grace to the humble."
>
> —James 4:6

> If my people who are called by my name humble themselves, and pray and seek my face and turn from their wicked ways, then I will hear from heaven and will forgive their sin and heal their land.
>
> —2 Chronicles 7:14

Jesus taught us to come as children (Matthew 18:3). Why? Because children don't carry all the baggage of personal accomplishments that we adults do. They come because they've been invited, not because they're worthy.

Have you ever heard of a café coronary? That's medical slang for a person dying of an airway obstructed by food.

Pride is a spiritual café coronary.

When I was in high school, my family took a trip to see my grandparents. I liked taking trips because it was a chance to eat out in restaurants. One Sunday afternoon, my family was eating together in a Howard Johnson's. I wanted dessert, but my father nixed it, saying I didn't need it. "And besides, money doesn't grow on trees."

(Hmm . . . how many times have I used that same line on my kids?)

A few moments later, I looked up to see an elderly man stagger to his feet, clutching at his throat. I pointed. "That man can't breathe!"

The next second my father, a family physician, was on his feet. He reached around the man from behind and performed a Heimlich maneuver, popping the offending pickle from the man's trachea. The man's life was saved, and I remember the pride I felt after watching my father in action.

When my father went to pay the bill, the manager refused to accept payment. My father had more than paid our debt by preventing a death in the restaurant.

What was my response? Looking back, I can see the gospel debt in my words.

"Since it was free, you should have let me get dessert."

Amazing. I went from thankful for a saved life to thinking about my own stomach at the speed of light. I'd like to say that was typical teenager behavior that I've outgrown, but the truth is, I can still slip from living in the sufficiency of grace (extending grace to others because I am living in acknowledgment of my own need for grace) to gospel debt in seconds.

But thankfully, just as quickly as a Heimlich maneuver can open an obstructed airway, acknowledging our need is the first step in opening up the floodgates holding back God's grace.

We've started the treatment solution for gospel debt. And the beginning is as easy as opening the avenue for God's grace to reach us again and again. Just bring your need. Recognize it. Jump off the precarious, propped-up box of self-sufficiency that you stand on.

Let's get out of the mud puddle and back into the ocean of grace. And we start along the journey with *A: Acknowledge your need.*

Of course, that's just the first step. Once the airway is open, we need to breathe in the oxygen for it to do any good. That's what the next chapter is about. *B* is for Breathing.

By the way, do you want to know what happened to Billy Dean? He spent a few days on a ventilator with his head swelled up like a balloon. But he recovered. When his swelling went down, the breathing tube keeping his airway open was removed. In time he became known as a folk hero of sorts. (What does this say about our present culture?) He even had a short article written about him in a biker magazine. Tough guy. Won't take anything from anyone, not even a rattlesnake.

Oh well, maybe he learned something from the event. Maybe he even tells his kids a bit of life's wisdom. "Never bite a rattlesnake."

For Further Reflection

1. Why does the Bible often combine the word *life* with the word *breath*?

2. "A is for Acknowledge your need." What is the significance of this first step in the ABC's of spiritual life? Do you find it easy or difficult to admit your need because of sin? Why is it so important to do so?

3. "Pride . . . completely shuts off the airway, the avenue for God's abundant grace to flow into our needy souls." How so? With what results? This doesn't take away your salvation, but what does it do to you?

4. In what ways do we expect the Holy Spirit to take a backseat while we do the driving? With what results?

5. Why did Jesus tell us to come to him as little children? What is it about children that you should imitate in your attitude toward God and his grace?

CHAPTER FIVE

B is for Breathing

love motorcycles.

There, the confession is out. In spite of my profession as a surgeon, I've had a love affair with two-wheeled travel since I was old enough to buy my first mini-bike from Lowe's. It had a two and a half horsepower engine, a red frame, and no shocks. It sure was bumpy. Perhaps my dad let me buy it in hopes that it might bounce some sense into my preadolescent brain, but all it did was whet my appetite for more.

So you can pretty much follow my growing up years by the motorcycles I owned. A Honda Z50. Then a Honda XR75. Then my first full-sized bike, a Penton Berkshire 100.

I have another confession to make. I must have been about twelve years old when I snuck into my older sister's room to peek at her diary. I suppose I was looking for secret information valuable for leverage in case she ever had anything on me. But I didn't find anything about secret love. I found out how fed up she was about my passion for motorcycles.

"All Harry Lee thinks about is motorcycles. I think he eats, sleeps, and breathes motorcycles," she wrote.

Well, Donna was right. And she used a pretty nice physiology metaphor for a fourteen-year-old girl. And thinking about breathing grace brought her metaphor back to me after all these years.

Motorcycles and eighteen-wheelers don't mix. At least not when they are forced to share the same square footage of asphalt.

Just ask David Keith. He was just a happy teenager on his motorcycle when a truck pulled into his path.

A single second changed David's life forever.

He was lying on the road, unable to breathe. But unbeknownst to him, in the car behind him was a trained emergency medical technician, who assisted David through those first critical minutes after his accident.

David's spinal cord was severed between the first and second cervical vertebrae, paralyzing him from the neck down. Now it's a tragedy to not be able to move your arms and legs, but that doesn't pose the immediate life-threatening problem. It's the paralysis of the diaphragm that kills you. Let me explain.

The most important muscle used in breathing isn't one of the chest muscles. Sure, they contribute to the process, but by far the diaphragm, the large strip of muscle separating the chest cavity from the abdominal cavity, is the most important. Your brain sends a message down the phrenic nerve: *Breathe!* The message then spreads as an impulse across the diaphragm, causing it to push downward toward the stomach and other abdominal organs. This lowers the pressure in the chest cavity, and air rushes into the lungs.

If the spinal cord is severed above the exit of the phrenic nerve, the nerve that carries the impulse to the diaphragm, the diaphragm is paralyzed. In medicine we have a little poem to help us remember the levels of the cervical spinal cord that supply portions of the phrenic nerve: "Three, four, and five keep the diaphragm alive."

Unfortunately for David, his spinal cord was severed well above the takeoff of his phrenic nerve. So his ability to breathe on his own was ended.

He had an open airway; there was no airway obstruction. But oxygen doesn't move into the lungs just because there isn't vocal cord swelling or some other airway problem. To move oxygen into the lungs where it can do some good requires breathing. And that's the *B* in the ABC's that guide physicians in resuscitation.

In the same way, just because we've opened our lives up to the gospel doesn't ensure that will be effective in relieving our spiritual pathology. We open the airway by acknowledging our need. Perhaps to extend the metaphor, I should call it a graceway instead of an airway. I like that. Pride obstructs the graceway.

Just because the graceway is open doesn't ensure that the gospel will be effective in doing its work. We need to move to the next step: *B* is for *believing the gospel.*

The gospel message is straightforward. I have been placed in right standing before a holy God, with full access to all the benefits of sonship. I don't deserve this, but it's mine nonetheless. Now this gospel wasn't given just to get me out of the hell I deserve. That was only the beginning. The principles that brought me into relationship with God are the same ones that enable the promises of the gospel to bring about their transforming work now that I'm his. Listen to what the Bible teaches.

> For by grace you have been saved *through faith*. And this
> is not your own doing; it is the gift of God, not a result
> of works, so that no one may boast.
>
> —Ephesians 2:8-9, emphasis added

> For God so loved the world, that he gave his only Son,
> that whoever *believes* in him should not perish but have
> eternal life.
>
> —John 3:16, emphasis added

> Therefore, since we have been justified *by faith*, we have
> peace with God through our Lord Jesus Christ.
>
> —Romans 5:1, emphasis added

OK, these are the basics. The promises of God for salvation are
only effective if we believe.

Believe. It's the *B* of the ABC's.

We've been saved because we acknowledged our need. In essence,
we recognized our sin. And then we believed the truth of the gospel.
But too many of us stop with an initial salvation experience. We came
to the cross, believed the message of salvation, and then went on with
our lives, facing the problems of life with only an infancy of faith.
The problem? Our understanding of the sufficiency of Christ's work
never kept pace with our understanding of God's holiness or our own
sinfulness. The result? Gospel debt! Look at the very next verse in the
fifth chapter of Romans.

> Through him we have also obtained access *by faith* into
> this grace in which we stand, and we rejoice in hope of
> the glory of God.
>
> —Romans 5:2, emphasis added

Not only have I been justified (Jesus' righteous deeds on my record
in place of my sin, the great switch) by faith, but I now access the

grace that allows me to walk forward as a son with this same belief. Remember Paul's encouragement to the believers in Colosse?

> Therefore, as you received Christ Jesus the Lord, so walk in him.
>
> —Colossians 2:6

How did we receive Christ? By faith.
Now how are we to walk? By faith.
Read the next verse.

> . . . rooted and built up in him and established *in the faith.*
>
> —Colossians 2:7, emphasis added

But to most of the church, faith remains an elusive concept. We stumble along, hearing about it but not really grasping its simplicity.

Ask most Christians to define it, and the definitions get tangled in circular thinking.

"Well, faith is believing."

"Believing is hoping."

"Hoping is trusting."

"Trusting is having faith."

Around and around we go.

Take a poll to find out what faith is, and at best you'll end up with a partial truth.

Many think of faith as magical electricity, something that needs to be worked up, like a basketball team psyching themselves up before a big game.[6] To many it's a spooky concept, something so nebulous that we cannot put our fingers around it and draw it into our daily experience.

The Bible defines it like this:

> Now faith is *the assurance* of things hoped for, *the conviction* of things not seen.
>
> —Hebrews 11:1, emphasis added

> Without faith it is impossible to please him, for whoever would draw near to God must believe that he exists and that he rewards those who seek him.
>
> —Hebrews 11:6

In fact, you need to re-read the whole eleventh chapter of Hebrews to realize that faith isn't faith apart from the actions that are accomplished through it. The entire "hall of fame of faith" as reported in that chapter is made up of people who *did something* by faith. And while you're reading about the heroes of faith, notice that their lives were hard and characterized by intense suffering, bearing little resemblance to the comfortable lives those in the western church think is their birthright as Christians.

What did James say?

> I will show you my faith by my works.
>
> —James 2:18b

Now the point of this isn't that faith is part of good works, and certainly not that salvation by faith is really some code name for salvation coming only to those who deserve it, work for it, and tip the scales in their favor.

Salvation is by grace alone. Period.

And faith alone. Period.

But saving faith produces fruit, in the same way that I can point to the grapefruit tree hanging in my front yard in Kijabe, Kenya and say, "It's a grapefruit tree." How do I know? I see the evidence. I can hold it in my hands. And I can taste the sour fruit with my tongue.

A life lived in a state of gospel debt is fruitless because by definition, faith in the gospel message results in action, fruit the world can taste and see.

What is faith? An assurance that prompts sinners into looking outside themselves for a solution.[7] It is a way of thinking that stimulates action. It is simply the conviction that the gospel is true. And the resulting action is to place our lives in God's hands.

OK, what does that mean? A conviction that the gospel is true is the recognition that we're not in control. We didn't earn it, work for it, or deserve it. So we rely on Christ. We lean on him. And believing that the gospel is true is what brings grace into our lives.

In future chapters we'll look in a bit more detail at the application of the ABC's to assist us out of a life of gospel debt. But for now I just want to drive home a basic concept. Believing the gospel is how we came to Christ. We believed. That prompted action. That action was simply looking to Christ to save us.[8] We leaned on him. We had the inner assurance that he alone held the solution. And this is the same way we are to respond to each situation in our lives when we find ourselves in gospel debt.

Remember that meddlesome review of systems we went through? Think of one small area of gospel debt as an illustration. I find myself anxious about an upcoming presentation. *I have so much to do and so little time. What if I can't remember what I wanted to say?* At that moment I'm functioning out of a gospel debt. I'm acting out of a false gospel of pride. When I am functioning in appropriate gospel saturation, I am treasuring Christ as the solution, and he gets the glory he deserves. When I am functioning out of my own pride, I'm worried about how I'll look to others. I'm the one being treasured, and I'm hoping I'll get the glory for giving a great presentation.

So I realize the problem: I'm anxious. That's the first step. *A*: I acknowledge my need. I see that I've been trying to bridge the gospel gap by trying to look good. That opens the graceway, the avenue for grace to enter my soul. But I still need to believe the message of the gospel for it to be effective in my life. I choose to believe that God is in charge of my salvation and every ongoing need in my life. He is the one who is at work, requiring only my need and my willingness to turn to him for a solution. It is this turning to him, this leaning on him to meet the need, that is the essence of step *B*: believing the gospel promises. In this case I could have gotten even more specific, pulling any number of promises from the Bible that deal with anxiety and choosing to believe.

> Therefore I tell you, do not be anxious about your life, what you will eat or what you will drink, nor about your body, what you will put on. Is not life more than food, and the body more than clothing? Look at the birds of the air; they neither sow nor reap nor gather into barns, and yet your heavenly Father feeds them. . . . Therefore do not be anxious about tomorrow.
>
> —Matthew 6:25-26, 34a

We look at the promise and believe, choosing to look to Christ for the solution instead of relying on ourselves. In effect, we've moved out of gospel debt and back into grace.

So what happened to David Keith? He's lived many years since the accident. And he's one of my heroes because he's chosen to embrace life in spite of the difficulties he's been handed.

He's permanently paralyzed (on this side of heaven, of course) from the neck down. He operates a motorized wheelchair with a sip-and-puff straw that allows him to direct the movements by applying a gentle suction or puff into the end of a tube. He can type twenty-five words a minute with a laser pointer attached to his head and a special computer screen.

It's been a few years since I've seen him, but the last I knew, he was in a competitive graduate school.

Oh yeah, I almost forgot. He lives because of a mechanical ventilator. Sure, he has an open airway for oxygen to get in, but he can't breathe on his own because his diaphragm is paralyzed. He can't talk unless the ventilator gives him a breath. That makes him seem contemplative in conversation. He speaks and then pauses, waiting for a rhythmic breath before continuing with his sentence. When the phone rings, the person on the other end needs to wait until David's respirator gives him a breath or he won't be able to say, "Hello." If they're impatient, not understanding his situation, they may hold for only a few seconds before hanging up. That's just one of the hundreds of inconveniences his paralysis has meant for him.

He has a permanent tracheostomy, a surgical airway created so a tube can enter straight into his windpipe at the front of his neck.

He has an open airway, but he can't breathe without help.

Many of us are like David. We know we have a need. The graceway is open. But we don't breathe it into our lives by simply believing the message.

For Further Reflection

1. What do you "eat, sleep, and breathe"? Why?

2. "Just because the graceway is open doesn't ensure that the gospel will be effective in doing its work." Why is this so? What is a graceway?

3. "B is for believing the gospel." What is the importance of this second step in the ABC's of spiritual life? What does it really mean to believe? What is the gospel?

4. What happens if your understanding of the sufficiency of Christ's work on the cross doesn't keep pace with your understanding of God's holiness or your own sinfulness? With what results?

5. What is faith? What is faith not? What does saving faith always produce?

CHAPTER SIX

C is for Circulation

f his parents could change places with Ben, I'm sure they would. In a heartbeat. Not because Ben won the lottery but because he has rheumatic heart disease. And I know his parents. Parents like Dan and Linda would gladly take the suffering of their child, even if it meant standing in his place.

Some would say it was just dumb luck. Or bad timing. Really bad timing. But I believe in God's sovereignty, the fact that God's love sometimes comes packaged in pain. So I can't say any of those things.

I remember the fall of 2003 at Rift Valley Academy in Kijabe, Kenya because an influenza virus cut a broad swath across the student body. In some classes only a few kids were well enough to continue.

The students were divided into "coughers" and "non-coughers" and were asked to eat at separate times in the cafeteria. Many, many kids were ill, set aside with fever, sore throat, runny noses, and vomiting. When we gathered for a church service, the coughing provided a kind of scratchy, rhythmic background noise. It was so constant that when it stopped, the silence was something you noticed.

One of my sons lost 10 percent of his body weight in two weeks.

And that's when Ben got sick. Right at the tail of the influenza outbreak. He went to the infirmary with flu symptoms, a sore throat, and a few nonspecific symptoms. In many ways he looked like so many of the other kids. The infirmary was out of stock on throat swab tests for strep. But a plan was in place: Watch things for a while; go to the hospital for a test if the sore throat continued. In light of the influenza outbreak, it was a good plan.

And Ben's sore throat went away.

But he just stayed so dog-tired. It got bad enough that a month later, while others were conditioning for rugby, just a sprint across the field would send Ben into a search for air.

His mom remembers his cough. She lifts a hand to her brown hair, and pain from the memory returns to her face. "You could tell he just wasn't normal."

Ben's parents are missionaries serving in an area in Africa where Islam enjoys a solid majority. They had made a difficult choice when they placed Ben in a missionary boarding school. They had some communication from him before he arrived to be with them during the December school break. He just couldn't seem to shake the fatigue left over from the flu.

But Dan, his father and a pediatrician, laid a stethoscope on his son's chest and recognized the problem immediately. Ben was in heart failure, his aortic valve destroyed by infection from streptococcal bacteria.

Have you ever wondered why strep throat seems like such a big deal to pediatricians? It has nothing to do with the throat. It has to do with the propensity of streptococcal bacteria to infect the heart valves.

What we think happened to Ben is that he was infected with strep throat that went untreated and resulted in endocarditis, an infection of his heart valves. In Ben's case, it destroyed his aortic valve.

Think back to high school biology with me for a moment. The aortic valve sits right at the outflow of the left ventricle, the big pumping chamber that receives oxygen-rich blood coming back from the lungs and propels it out through the aortic valve into the aorta and the rest of the body. The aortic valve keeps the blood flowing in one direction, away from the heart and into the oxygen-needy body. But not so for Ben, whose aortic valve had been nibbled away with infection. In such a case, instead of allowing the blood to only go in one direction, the blood propelled into the aorta drops back into the left ventricle when it relaxes between pumps. But remember, blood is also running into the left ventricle, fresh from the lungs. So the ventricle grows bigger to deal with the extra volume. And eventually it is overstretched and can't pump effectively. Blood backs up into the lungs, producing a wet cough and fatigue. For a while patients are OK when they are resting, but just exercise a little bit, even something minor, and the body demands more oxygen. How do we deliver more? We breathe faster; our heart rate increases. But that creates problems for the heart in failure. It can't keep up and will fail more as a consequence. Eventually the patient can't breathe, even at rest, and a cycle of worsening failure is established, like the circling of vultures lowering slowly over their next meal.

Dan's own heart sank as he listened to the striking heart murmur in his son. It was time for action. His firstborn son was in circulatory failure in the middle of primitive Africa.

All of the cells in our body, all one hundred trillion of them, need oxygen to survive. Some are more resilient than others, capable of some compensation when oxygen tensions drop below normal. Other cells, like the brain, need a steady, moment-by-moment supply. The lungs bring it in. The carrying of oxygen into the blood takes place, but it won't get out where it's needed without a pump. That, of course, brings us to *C*: Circulation. In an emergency situation, once the airway is open and breathing has been initiated, we have to be sure the oxygen will be circulated to every starving cell crying for attention.

At the cellular level, metabolic processes—molecular chemical reactions—are ongoing, even during sleep. It's a process by which oxygen is taken in and used up in chemical reactions and carbon dioxide is given off as a byproduct. This process is called cellular respiration. Without a constant supply, much of the cellular metabolic processes revert to plan B, a set of inefficient reactions to produce a little energy. After a few minutes without oxygen, cells begin to die.

The brain dies first. It's unfortunate really. It's like the commander-in-chief taking the first hit and all the infantry men surviving to fight it out by themselves without a leader.

The truth is, we need grace on a moment-to-moment basis just as much as we need oxygen. It's just not as obvious. But just as every cell needs oxygen for efficient function, so every part of our social, emotional, mental, and spiritual life needs to be bathed in grace.

Continually. Grace every hour.

Every second.

We need grace to stay out of gospel debt. To avoid dropping into inefficiency like cells trying to make energy without oxygen.

Did you know that a heartbeat can be detected just twelve weeks after conception? And that amazing muscle keeps right on beating until the other extreme of life when we step out of this shell and into eternity. It never takes a break because it's tired. It just keeps on going and going and going. And when it stops, we use its last beat to define the time of death.

Why continuously? Because our body demands oxygen continuously.

What's harder to realize is that our need for continuous gospel truths, our need for a rhythmic pulsing of grace through every part of our lives, is just as real.

The Bible teaches us to

> . . . grow in the grace and knowledge of our Lord and
> Savior Jesus Christ.
>
> —2 Peter 3:18

Notice that the grace that brought us salvation isn't to be once sampled and then set aside. We are to grow in grace, and this growth in grace needs to parallel our growth of the knowledge of God. That's why Peter said, "Grow in . . . grace and knowledge." Otherwise we find ourselves in a grace or gospel debt, and our spiritual cellular metabolism falls into disarray.

One of the main points of metabolism is the creation of the energy-storage molecule known by the initials ATP. When oxygen is available, ATP is made efficiently through a complicated series of steps called the Krebs cycle that all medical students have to memorize. Don't ask me why. I never use it now! When oxygen isn't available, a few ATP are made, but nothing like during times of oxygen-plenty. And the energy from these reactions is what provides the fuel for just about everything else.

Where am I going with this? By now you are learning the metaphor that is at the heart of this book. If you want to have the energy to run a spiritual race, you need to stay saturated with grace.

And it's not enough to acknowledge your need and believe. Grace needs adequate exposure to every area of your life, and that means circulation.

C is for communion.

There are gospel truths, gospel promises, that we need to keep in constant focus. Truths like . . . this is God's work. He's in control. He's the one who gets the glory.

And, he wants his love to reach every darkened corner of our lives. Every hurt. Every anxiety.

There is no wound that cannot be soothed by the salve of his love. There is no anxious thought that can't be quieted by his touch. There is no hurt too deep for his love to cover, no sin so despicable that he cannot forgive, no panic that he cannot quell, no runaway emotion that he cannot rein in.

But healing takes exposure. A constant circulation of gospel truth. Circulation means communion. Time alone in quietness. Solitude.[9]

It's a discipline that has been forgotten and shoved aside by a church consumed with doing.

Have you ever taken a day just with your Bible and not talked to anyone except your Heavenly Father? Just you and your Father, his Word and no agenda.

Time spent just listening.

Boy, that sounds like a waste of time.

The point is, grace penetration takes time. Time spent in his presence. Time away from cell phones, pagers, and all other interruptions.

And you need to persist, even when your mind is waging war against your plan.[10] *I have so much to do. Time alone is selfish. I should be with my family. I should be writing. I should be . . . I should be . . . I should be . . .*

Think for a moment about how you determine your worth. Most of us men are tempted to define our worth through our work, accomplishments, or career. This, of course, is true for women as well, but I believe men are a bit more prone to this distraction. For students, it may be your grades. Perhaps it's your looks, your money, your car or your house, or your value to your coworkers. Perhaps you define your worth through your children or grandchildren. Maybe you define your value through your skill as an artist or your way with words. What kind of measuring sticks do you hold up to your life to say, "I'm OK"? We all have them, and we tend to use them constantly.

Most of us like to hang around people who make us feel good about ourselves. And fellowship with others is a major means of grace delivery in our lives. We'll look more at that in a later chapter. But there is a temptation when we're with others. It's the temptation to hold up the measuring stick in judgment of our brothers and sisters. For some of us, this is a fine art: compare, compare, compare. And if someone doesn't quite measure up, we feel a bit better about ourselves.

But when we spend time in solitude—just us and God—the measuring sticks we use to calculate our worth look pretty puny beside his greatness. We need to stay in his presence until we stop judging ourselves by our measuring sticks. In his presence only one thing matters: him! The magnitude of his holiness, his power, and his grace quickly overwhelm even our proudest accomplishments or attainments. And it is only when we have learned to stop continuously measuring our worth with man-made constructions that we can stop judging our brothers.[11]

Usually that's the point at which grace, not judgment, takes a front seat in our relationships. When we've persisted in circulating God's grace to every area of our lives, those around us reap the benefits, because grace naturally overflows when our souls are filled with his gospel.

When we've laid aside our measuring sticks in the presence of God, how do we determine our worth? Like he does. On the basis of what he paid to purchase our salvation. We are precious to him because his Son died to pay the price for our sin. Learning to define ourselves as children of God and not by our own measuring sticks takes time spent in his Word, time in adoration of our Father.[12]

I love to grill, but that means preparation. The meat has to marinate for hours to take on the flavors of the sauce. And my life needs grace-marinating to exude the grace of God to others around me.

We need exposure to his Word every day. That's why he gave manna to the children of Israel a day at a time. To remind them daily of their need for him.

But we seem naturally wired to forget. That's why he doesn't give us one dose of grace at salvation and then leave us to coast.

There are no extended grace preparations. In real life, grace seems to have a short half-life. It needs to be dosed frequently to stay effective against soul infection.

In the pharmaceutical world, extended preparations are all the rage. No one wants to take four pills daily when you can engineer one that will do the job when dosed once a day. Most of them are called extended-release. But God doesn't give grace that way. He gives grace at the point of our need, and it doesn't have a long half-life. That means we need frequent dosing to maintain an adequate level of circulating grace in our lives.

We can draw an interesting principle from the book of Isaiah:

> "To whom will he teach knowledge,
> and to whom will he explain the message?
> Those who are weaned from the milk,
> those taken from the breast?
> For it is precept upon precept, precept upon precept,
> line upon line, line upon line,
> here a little, there a little."

> —Isaiah 28:9-10

This gets repetitive for a reason. "Precept upon precept, precept upon precept, line upon line, line upon line." It's because there is no wholesale storehouse for grace. Yes, it is in endless supply. That's not my point. The point is that we need minute-by-minute dosing!

Ask most Christians if they believe a particular gospel truth, say the principle that nothing they can do would make them more acceptable to God, and they will say, "Yes." But the truth is not played out in their day-to-day life. When the rubber hits the road, they still operate out of a works-gospel, feeling like they're just a little more lovable if they manage to share their faith or give money to a bell-ringer in front of Wal-Mart at Christmas. So the airway may be open. They even breathed in the truth by believing. But it takes regular circulation and exposure for some truths to take.

Jesus used another metaphor that helps bring this into sharper focus.

> Abide in me, and I in you. As the branch cannot bear fruit by itself, unless it abides in the vine, neither can you, unless you abide in me. I am the vine; you are the branches. Whoever abides in me and I in him, he it is that bears much fruit, for apart from me you can do nothing.
>
> —John 15:4-5

Abide. Stay in his presence.

> . . . his delight is in the law of the LORD,
> and on his law he meditates day and night.
> He is like a tree
> planted by streams of water
> that yields its fruit in its season,
> and its leaf does not wither.
> In all that he does, he prospers.
>
> —Psalm 1:2-3

"Meditate" day and night. And this isn't referring to emptying your mind, as in eastern religious technique. It's chewing and re-chewing the same verses, much like a cow ruminating on partially digested grass. It brings it up over and over. Not the most pleasant metaphor, but it works.

Isaiah got repetitive for a reason. Repetition imprints knowledge in the human cortex. And now that we've covered another initial, we need to go back to the beginning.

A is for *acknowledge our need*. It's the airway, the access that allows the gospel truth into our lives. Pride is this step's nemesis.

B is for *believing the gospel*. This is simply accepting the gospel truths for what they are and turning to Christ for a solution.

C is for *communion*, circulation of the gospel truths to give every aspect of our souls the appropriate time of exposure to grace.

Airway. Breathing. Circulation.

Acknowledge your need.

Believe the gospel.

Communion.

What happened to Ben? We last left him with heart failure in remote Africa. Fortunately for Ben, his father recognized the problem and facilitated an air evacuation to Johannesburg, South Africa.

There he was evaluated by a pediatric cardiologist and was found to have aortic valve regurgitation. That's what we call it when blood crosses back and forth across a one-way valve. He was treated for heart failure with medications, and a year later, when he was back in the United States, he underwent open-heart surgery for correction of his valve problem.

Heart failure is terrifying. The lungs fill with fluid backing up from the heart, producing white, frothy sputum like bubbly sea foam. But thanks to a gracious God, Ben recovered.

I ate Christmas dinner with Ben this year. Like most teenagers, he doesn't talk much about his heart problem. He's moved on, probably more concerned about college and his dating life.

Remarkably, in spite of their trial, Ben's family is still in Africa, faithfully serving the One who called them. After all, giving out the life of the gospel once you've taken it in is a natural spiritual respiration. Grace in. Grace out.

But we'll get to that in a later chapter.

For Further Reflection

1. "C is for communion." What is the importance of this third step in the ABC's of spiritual life? What is communion in this sense, and how do we experience it on an ongoing basis?

2. "There is no wound that cannot be soothed by the salve of [God's] love. There is no anxious thought that can't be quieted by his touch. There is no hurt too deep for his love to cover, no sin so despicable that he cannot forgive, no panic that he cannot quell, no runaway emotion that he cannot rein in." Is this just wishful thinking, or is this really true? How do you know it's true?

3. How do you remain in continuing fellowship with God? Have you ever taken a significant amount of time to just be alone with God and his Word? With what results? When will you do this again (or perhaps for the first time)?

4. How can you measure your true worth? What measuring sticks do you need to set aside? How does God tell you your worth before him?

5. "Grace seems to have a short half-life. It needs to be dosed frequently to stay effective against soul infection." What does this mean? How do you need to apply this in your life?

CHAPTER SEVEN

Using the ABC's in College

I was the only general surgeon around the day a truck rear-ended a bus and rolled off the road near the mission hospital in Kijabe, Kenya.

Most of the passengers on the bus were fine. But the truck's occupants were the problem. You see, in Africa the main mode of transportation is the feet. If you're lucky, perhaps a truck might be going your way, and the driver will certainly be kind enough to let you climb aboard. On this particular day thirty Maasai tribesmen and women climbed aboard the back of a tall truck carrying seventy goats.

When I was in surgery residency, we had a name for the injuries sustained when someone fell out of the back of a pickup. We just started calling them FOOT injuries, for Fell Out Of Truck. But at the most, from one accident you might see two or three.

Well, on that day, after the dust and blood had been cleaned from the Casualty Department floor, we had treated thirty-four patients from one accident.

Another thing about Kenya that you need to understand is that there is no pre-hospital care. No one arrives neatly packaged on a backboard with a cervical collar and IV's running. Most of them are carried in or thrown in the back of yet another vehicle and rushed to the hospital by some roadside Good Samaritan.

In fact, when we were attending orientation school in preparation for serving with Africa Inland Mission, they told us to carry a shower curtain along in our vehicle.

"What on earth for?"

"It will keep your car from getting bloody when you pick up a car-accident victim."

Right. How common could that be?

Common, I soon found out. In fact, I have picked up a roadside victim in Africa before, but that's another story . . .

You need to imagine the scene in Casualty that day. Casualty is the Kenyan word for emergency room. At our hospital, Casualty is basically one big room lined with stretchers. That day there was a bleeding body in every bed, and patients who needed stretchers sat on benches waiting for someone to die or be treated and moved to a hospital bed so they could lie down.

Maasai are tough. They don't cry when they're in pain. They were all in traditional dress, and none of them spoke a language we could understand. And they just kept coming.

So how did we decide whom to treat first?

I know you at least suspect the answer. It's a process called triage, a French word meaning "to sort." Those who are not salvageable, you skip over. That's the hardest thing to do. That day I only skipped over one. The ones who are most critical get seen first. So I went bed to bed, making assessments and sorting them *according to the ABC's.*

Imagine you're the intern assigned to one patient. By now you know the drill. Priority number one is airway. That accessed, you move on to *B* and *C*. Thirty minutes later you've gotten all the X-rays you need; you've made a diagnosis of three left rib fractures, a pelvic fracture, a scalp laceration, and a left ankle sprain.

You sit for a moment to complete your admission orders when the nurse informs you, "His blood pressure is 60."

What do you do? The patient isn't behaving the way you wanted. You've already finished the ABC's. In fact, you were well beyond *D* (disability) and *E* (expose) and minutes from getting a needed cup of java.

The answer? *You go back to the ABC's!*

The ABC's are repeated every time the patient takes a dive.

You assess the airway. You look at his respiratory effort. It has definitely worsened. He is struggling a bit and is taking shallow breaths.

You lay your stethoscope on his chest. *There is no air movement on the side of the rib fractures. A rib has probably punctured the lung.*

The situation is an urgent one. Air that the patient breathes in escapes through a tear in the air sacs of the lung and collects outside the lung, slowly filling up the chest cavity and compressing the lung and eventually the heart, causing a fall in blood pressure. You make the diagnosis and insert a chest tube to relieve the buildup of air.

To the trauma surgeon, airway, breathing, and circulation checks become reflexive, an automatic response when anything goes wrong. The whole point I want to drive home here is that the ABC's of spiritual resuscitation should become reflexive as well.

Every day.

Every hour.

Walter Payton, Hall of Fame running back for the Chicago Bears, ran with the football for over eight miles. That doesn't sound so impressive, does it? We've probably all seen marathon runners. They do over three times that distance every race.

But Walter Payton got knocked down every three or four yards by guys who weighed three hundred pounds.

The Christian life has often been compared to a race. That's even a biblical metaphor. But realize it's not just about distance. It's about falling every few steps and getting back up again. We're human. Over and over and over again we fall.

And each time we need to turn to the ABC's to pull us out of the gospel debt we're in. It needs to become an automatic response, something we do so quickly that it's as *natural as breathing*.

> Through him then let us continually offer up a sacrifice of praise to God, that is, the fruit of lips that acknowledge his name.
>
> —Hebrews 13:15

"Continually." Like breathing. Like a reflex. Notice what the writer says: ". . . the fruit of lips that acknowledge his name." The first step out of gospel debt is always the same. We have to see our need to open the way to help. And lips that acknowledge their need and acknowledge his name are on the path where the abundant grace of the cross is cherished.

The ABC's aren't steps that we follow one time in patient care and then move on to bigger and better things. Likewise, repentance, faith in God's promises, and circulation of the gospel into every area of our lives are steps to be returned to over and over and over. Every three or four yards. Every time we get upended by one of life's three-hundred-pound temptations.

The letters of the alphabet, our ABC's as we called them in kindergarten, aren't something we learn once and then move on. Been there.

Done that. Took the test. We use the alphabet in kindergarten and in every subsequent grade.

The ABC's of spiritual respiration are to be part of our day-to-day lives. That's why breathing grace is such a great metaphor. It's something we need to practice continuously.

> Rejoice always, pray without ceasing, give thanks in all circumstances; for this is the will of God in Christ Jesus for you.
>
> —1 Thessalonians 5:16-18

"Always." "Without ceasing." "In all circumstances." It's God's will. Wow. God must know something about our need that we're blind to.

I have a natural tendency to fight tooth-and-nail—the inclination to hide from the light when I'm dirty. When we have need for grace, our tendency is to clean ourselves up a little so we feel good enough to approach God.

I can't pray now. I just yelled at the kids.

But as soon as we see our need, we need to believe and come. "Just as I am, without one plea," you know?

> For we do not have a high priest who is unable to sympathize with our weaknesses, but one who in every respect has been tempted as we are, yet without sin. Let us then with confidence draw near to the throne of grace, that we may receive mercy and find grace to help in time of need.
>
> —Hebrews 4:15-16

Notice when we're encouraged to come? In our "time of need." And how? "With confidence." Not slinking in but boldly drawing in when we need grace and mercy.

Our tendency is to come when we're on top of our spiritual game, after a touchdown. But we want to hide from the coach in the locker room if we've been tackled behind the line of scrimmage or fumbled the ball.

Remember when King David sent Joab and the commanders of his army out to number the people of Israel (2 Samuel 24; 1 Chronicles 21)? This act, taking a census to find out how many capable fighting men were in Israel, brought on quite a reaction from the Almighty. David got to choose his punishment: three years of famine, three months of devastation by enemies, or three days of pestilence from an angelic sword.

David chose door number three, and seventy thousand men of Israel fell by the sword of the Lord!

Come on, God! What was the big deal? All he did was count his men!

Evidently it *was* a big deal. A huge deal. Why? Because men always want to rely on their own strength. David would have been tempted to take credit for victories in battle because of the size of his army.

It is this tendency to do it ourselves, to rely on our own resources, to want to be rewarded for our goodness, to be praised when everything works that sits at the core of the false works-gospel that traps so many of us in gospel debt and keeps us from the grace flow that's available. The ABC's help us take our focus off ourselves and put it back on the source of grace himself.

We're closing this first section. We've been through the ABC's of resuscitation and have seen that to stay out of our natural inclination toward gospel debt, we need the ABC's not only at salvation but every day, every hour.

That's why I called this chapter "Using the ABC's in College." I need a reminder that although we doctors learned the ABC's early, we keep using them throughout our career. So also with the spiritual principles I've presented here. In my walk with Christ, I should never move beyond the realm of realizing my need of grace, believing the gospel, and communing with him to allow the truth to penetrate my heart.

Because of days like the one where we treated dozens of Maasai tribesmen from one bus accident, the trauma ABC's have become reflexive for me. My prayer for you (and for myself since I am as needy as you) is that the ABC's of spiritual life will become reflexive too. Every day may our appreciation of God's holiness grow, our understanding of our own depravity without Christ deepen, and our comprehension of the power of the cross to swell to bridge the gap!

For Further Reflection

1. The ABC's need to be repeated whenever a patient takes a turn for the worse. How does this relate to the ABC's of the spiritual life?

2. How does Walter Payton's perseverance on the football field need to be paralleled in your walk with God?

3. "I have a natural tendency to fight tooth-and-nail—the inclination to hide from the light when I'm dirty. When we have need for grace, our tendency is to clean ourselves up a little so we feel good enough to approach God." Can you identify with this? Why would you rather hide than confess and keep going? How can you avoid relying on yourself rather than on the Lord?

4. Why was David's counting his fighting men such an offense to God? What might be a counterpart in your life?

5. How can you get to the point where the ABC's of the spiritual life will become reflexive? How can we help each other experience a triumphant "comprehension of the power of the cross"?

PART TWO

Problems:
What Happens
When Respiration Fails

CHAPTER EIGHT

Spiritual Emphysema

Do me a favor. Hold your breath. Seriously. Right now. Hold your breath as long as you can. I just did it while I was writing this. After only five seconds I felt the initial stirrings that I should take a breath. After thirty seconds my mind was sending a constant message: *GET AIR!* After one minute my lungs felt like they were going to explode.

Nothing else around me mattered. My wife was sitting nearby. I love her, but I wasn't thinking about her as I held my breath. Some of my favorite things were close to me within the living room of the little mission house in Kijabe. Books of much-loved authors lined the shelves. A DVD series I enjoy, a comfortable chair, and my laptop computer were there. But nothing mattered to me while I was holding my breath. My mind first whispered, then screamed, then threatened hostile takeover, demanding I give in to the order: *BREATHE!*

The feeling of needing air is immediate. Terrifying. And if any of you have ever gotten into trouble underwater, it is something you're not likely to forget in this lifetime.

But it's not the lack of oxygen that drives us to breathe. It's the buildup of carbon dioxide, the by-product of cellular respiration. As soon as we stop breathing, the CO_2 level in the bloodstream starts rising, stimulating receptors within the brain. Immediately the signals go out: *Breathe faster! Lower the CO_2!*

A dangerous practice takes place every summer in swimming pools all over America. Some teenager is in a breath-holding contest. He intentionally hyperventilates before diving under the water. What this does physiologically is to drive the carbon dioxide levels way below normal so that it takes longer for them to rise up to the level when the you've-got-to-breathe-*now* signals are felt the strongest. This allows the hyperventilated teenager to hold his breath longer and win the contest.

There's just one problem with this: death.

That's right, death. Remember, while we're not breathing, not only does the CO_2 level rise, but the oxygen level falls, eventually to dangerous levels. At critically low oxygen levels, the teen will faint because of a lack of oxygen in the brain. And when a person faints underwater, reflexive breathing kicks in, and water is drawn into the lungs, resulting in drowning.

Physiology is the study of how the body works. Pathology is the study of how disease affects how the body works. In our search for a physiological metaphor for our need of grace, oxygen is perfect because our need for it is constant. And when the respiratory system goes wrong, our metaphor can provide new springboards of insight into spiritual pathology as well.

I'm sure you've seen people with end-stage chronic obstructive pulmonary disease (COPD), maybe at a mall, riding a little motorized wheelchair, never far from a green oxygen tank. They exhale through pursed lips and get breathless at minimal exertion. One thing that's different about them is something you can't see. Their drive to breathe isn't due to carbon dioxide; it's due to low oxygen—exactly opposite from a normal person. You see, a person with COPD or emphysema has a long-standing partial obstruction to the flow of air out of the lungs. Remember, we breathe in oxygen and breathe out carbon dioxide. When a person has difficulty with long-standing obstruction, the carbon dioxide levels in the bloodstream build up slowly to levels that are quite high, way above the levels that would stimulate a normal person to breathe faster.

What happens is that because the CO_2 levels rise slowly, the person with emphysema stops responding to the high CO_2 by breathing faster. They don't breathe faster until the oxygen levels are low enough to make them do so.

An interesting part of this is that the brain compensates quickly for rising CO_2 by increasing the respiratory rate. But after a few days there is a diminished respiratory response to the high CO_2. Do you see where this is leading?

Patients with COPD or emphysema have lost their sensitivity to the carbon dioxide.

This presents an interesting dilemma for the physician treating patients with COPD. You can't just slap them on oxygen like you would a normal patient because as soon as you raise the oxygen levels enough, the drive to breathe goes away, and they just forget to breathe!

So far in our look at respiration as a metaphor for taking in the gospel, we've looked at the oxygen side of the matter. But respiration serves two functions. It provides us with oxygen, and it gets rid of CO_2. When CO_2 builds up, it reeks all sorts of havoc. The blood gets acidic. The heart doesn't like that and eventually beats erratically and then stops altogether.

When someone overdoses on heroin or some other powerful narcotic, the respiratory center in the brain is targeted, effectively suppressing the drive to breathe. CO_2 builds up, inducing first sleepiness and then deep coma. A physician must act fast to breathe for the patient and then administer a narcotic antagonist, the antidote that can counter the overdose.

Have you noticed how unpopular it is to call sin sin? Homosexuality is "an alternative lifestyle." Adultery is an "affair." An angry person is "temper-challenged." Pornography is acceptable as long as it is wrapped in a popular sports magazine and called "the swimsuit edition." Gossip wears the jacket of "prayer concern." We hide our stinginess beneath a blanket of "stewardship." *I can give more later if my investments pay off.*

Lies are softened, bleached by new titles. A lie isn't a lie as long as it is a "white" one. What Jesus called adultery of the heart is only an "evil thought." Fornication and using the Lord's name in vain are now "adult situations" and "adult language."

Two generations ago, divorce carried a huge social stigma. Today divorce is common in and out of the church, accepted as a consequence of bad decisions and bad judgment.

Alcoholism is familial, due to faulty genes or abusive parents, certainly not to a lack of self-control.

Criminals are victims of poverty. Child-molesters are products of abuses they suffered as children themselves.

Society warms itself at the hearth of the victim mentality. We can't be responsible if we have our parents or our government to blame.

People with spiritual emphysema have lost their sensitivity to sin and its consequences.

How easy it is for me to call gray what was clearly black a few years ago. Have we slipped from stark contrasts of white and black into smudgy colors that are neither? Could it be that we are suffering from a spiritual malady no less serious than physical emphysema?

Recognition of sin and acknowledging our need of grace are to be regular respirations of our Christian experience. As we move forward, closer to the Father's heart, slowly more of our own sinfulness is revealed. At that point we face the problem of our unworthiness. How can we stand before a holy God? As long as our spiritual airway is opened by acknowledging our need and repenting, our recognition of his grace will more than fill the gap.

But too often we fall into sin and pull back into shame, and slowly our sensitivity to sin is dulled.

The first lie is the hardest. So is the first look at a pornographic Internet site. So is the first time we stretched a story to show ourselves in a favorable light. Soon we tumble down the slippery slope.

A high CO_2 level leads to acidosis, cardiac dysrhythmia, and death.

Spiritual emphysema leads to deepening gospel debt, self-justification, broken fellowship, and spiritual famine.

Just as carbon dioxide is cleansed from our cells every moment by breathing, so repentance needs to be part of our moment-by-moment walk with Christ in order to rid ourselves of the toxins that threaten our spiritual maturity. Repentance can be thought of as giving up our life for his. My wants are laid aside. My needs can no longer demand first place. It can't be about me, my pleasure, my future, my comfort, and my happiness. Repentance is turning from self-service to Christ's service, from loving me to treasuring Christ in all that he is. Luke tells us that Jesus called this dying to self and said it needed to be a part of our everyday experience.

> If anyone would come after me, let him deny himself and take up his cross daily and follow me.
> —Luke 9:23

Paul echoes the metaphor.

> I die every day!
> —1 Corinthians 15:31

The beauty of a life lived in the respiration of grace in, sin out is that this is where true joy makes its home. As I die to myself, my awareness of God's grace can explode to satisfy the very hunger that drove me into sin. Remember, sin is really only seeking satisfaction from a source outside of Christ and outside the immeasurable riches of his grace.

But just as rising carbon dioxide levels eventually result in a diminished respiratory response, so dwelling in sin results in an increased tolerance to sin. Seeing your own sin can be difficult. The longer I live, the more I see how easy it is for me to overlook my own problems in my survey of everyone else's evil. Jesus put his finger on the problem:

> Why do you see the speck that is in your brother's eye, but do not notice the log that is in your own eye? How can you say to your brother, "Brother, let me take out the speck that is in your eye," when you yourself do not see the log that is in your own eye? You hypocrite, first take the log out of your own eye, and then you will see clearly to take out the speck that is in your brother's eye.
>
> —Luke 6:41-42

We play in the mud puddle and criticize the river in which our neighbors delight. And as we judge our brothers, we ourselves are in gospel debt. Our pride has closed the graceway. We sit on our self-constructed judgment seat, graceless and blind.

So we find ourselves in a common predicament. By now you understand the treatment prescriptions. Turn to the ABC's—open the airway, believe the gospel, and settle into communion while you abide in God's grace. As we commune in his Word, a transformation begins to take place, and holiness is the result.

> I have stored up your word in my heart, that I might not sin against you.
>
> —Psalm 119:11

> And we all, with unveiled face, beholding the glory of the
> Lord, are being transformed into the same image from one
> degree of glory to another. For this comes from the Lord
> who is the Spirit.
>
> —2 Corinthians 3:18

We become what we behold. As my children watch and rewatch their favorite DVDs, their speech takes on the flavor of the characters they admire. As I spend time beholding the character of God (circulation of grace), I am changed "from one degree of glory to another." But if I wallow in self-pity or exult in self-worship, I am changed from one degree of misery to another into the image I behold: myself!

Yesterday one of my friends laughed at Samuel, my youngest son. He was describing how he had eaten a chocolate candy bar that had been melted in the African heat. "I made an incision in the top of the wrapper and sucked it out," he explained.

My friend thought his language was hilarious, but to Sam, his choice of words came directly from time spent with his surgeon father. Naturally he made an incision—he didn't just tear a hole in the wrapper. My point? Simply that we take on the characteristics of speech and action, good or bad, from those we spend time with and focus on. If I focus on Christ, I will slowly take on his attributes. If I focus on me, I become more like me—and I've had about enough of that. I want to be like Jesus!

Fortunately for us, God does not reveal the depth of our own need all at one time. Look closely at that last sentence. I've just caught myself calling sin *need*. Oh, how easy it is to be seduced by a politically correct society! Let me backtrack. God does not reveal the depth of our *sinfulness* all at one time. My father used to say that God deals with our sinful nature much as one would peel an onion—one layer at a time. God is the perfect chef, knowing just what we can stand and what would result in tears.

This brings us to a basic characteristic of God's grace. It is not a yardstick that is held up to show our shortcomings but a platform that facilitates our transformation. Unlike the law, which only points to the problem, grace provides the solution.

> For the grace of God has appeared, bringing salvation for all people, training us to renounce ungodliness and worldly passions, and to live self-controlled, upright, and godly lives in the present age.
>
> —Titus 2:11-12

How does grace facilitate the change? It refocuses us on God's provision. He can do what I can't. Remember what I contributed to my salvation? Nothing but my need. It was God's work start to finish. And what of the work of transformation? Again it's all a work of God, facilitated by his grace, accomplished only by an *acknowledgment* of our need, a *belief* in his provision, and time spent in *communion* with Christ.

Because emphysema is due to chronic airway obstruction, one component of therapy is often directed to an opening of the small airways. These medicines are known as bronchial dilators since they relax and expand the small bronchioles. For those of us with spiritual emphysema, a frequent dosing of a spiritual bronchial is the Rx.

The prescription should be written as follows: Use repentance as a constant infusion as needed for treatment of grace debt.

For Further Reflection

1. Why do you sometimes lose your sensitivity to sin? Why is this dangerous? Why do you find it so easy to call sin by some other name?

2. What is repentance? How does it relate to your own wants or comforts? To dying to self?

3. "As I die to myself, my awareness of God's grace can explode to satisfy the very hunger that drove me into sin." Is this an accurate assessment? How can divine grace satisfy a sinful hunger?

4. What mud puddles do you keep playing in? What rivers are you forgoing because you prefer the puddles? Why do you do this?

5. "God's grace . . . is not a yardstick that is held up to show our shortcomings but a platform that facilitates our transformation. Unlike the law, which only points to the problem, grace provides the solution." Explain. Does it sometimes feel like God is just finding fault? What is he really up to?

CHAPTER NINE

Spiritual Anemia:

When the Mailmen Go on Strike

At sixty, Margaret Johnson wasn't used to sitting down when her granddaughter skated in the park. But the winter of 2001 had dealt her a severe bout of the flu, and her recovery had been slow. She'd even joined the wellness center, figuring she was just out of shape. But after an embarrassing two minutes on the treadmill, she was leaning over the electronic console panting like she'd just run a marathon. She worried that she might disappoint her husband who had planned a spring trip to the Canadian Rockies. In nearly forty years of marriage she'd never let him out-hike her before. But unless something drastic happened, this was going to be the year.

She tried Power Bars and energy drinks and even a vitamin designed for the silver years, but nothing seemed to put the zip back in her step. It was time for a checkup, and after a month's wait she was finally on an exam table with her family doctor.

"I just need to get in shape. I guess I'm not forty anymore." She giggled.

Dr. Devin frowned as he looked at her fingernails and then pulled gently on her lower eyelid. "Are you having black stools?"

She shrugged. "Some, but I'm on a vitamin with iron. It must be that."

She didn't like the way the doctor said, "Hmmm" after each little portion of her exam.

After the exam, she frowned back at him. "You should never play poker."

He squinted his eyes in an expression of curiosity.

"You're concerned. I can see it on your face. You could never bluff me in a card game."

He chuckled. "I'm sure I wouldn't try." He sat in a padded chair and closed her chart. "We need to do some tests. And I want to send you to a surgeon."

"A surgeon?"

He nodded. "Only for some tests. I am going to ask Dr. Kraus to do a colonoscopy."

Her sister had been through that procedure. From her description, Margaret thought she'd rather pass.

"Your resting heart rate is 120. You're pale as a sheet."

"I haven't gotten any sun this winter. This flu has—"

"This is more than the flu, Margaret. And you're not pale because you need a tan. I found blood in the stool. I'm certain you're anemic."

Anemic? She'd heard of that too. Something old people took Geritol for. Old people were always at least ten years older than she was.

The doctor stood. "I've ordered a blood test. I'll have the scoop on your hemoglobin today."

Margaret went home after her lab test and waited by the phone. An hour later the answer was in. "Your hemoglobin level is 5."

"Five? Is that good?"

"Normal is over twice that." She listened as the doctor sighed into the phone. "It's no wonder you're tired. Your heart is working overtime to make up for the lack of red blood cells. I want you to have a blood transfusion—today. You could have a heart attack if your heart has to work much harder."

When I was in surgical training, I had a trauma surgery attending named Dr. Kearney. The residents loved him because he was passionate about teaching. He would constantly quiz us on the pathophysiology we saw in our patients, and he was quick with a zing if you answered incorrectly. "You've got a point, Harry," he would say, "but if you comb your hair, nobody will notice."

Surgeons like to think in simple terms. So they try to find appropriate examples to help them remember what they need to when they're sleep-deprived and in a life-or-death situation. Dr. Kearney was no different. He used the mailmen analogy to teach us about anemia.

"Think about what happens when there aren't enough mailmen. Maybe half of them go on strike, OK? The people in the town still need to get the mail, but now we're facing a shortage of delivery guys. They can't each carry more mail because their baskets are only so big. So in order to deliver all the mail, they have to travel *faster* in order to do the same total amount of work."

It's like that in anemia except the mailmen are hemoglobin molecules, and the mail is oxygen. The heart has to pump faster when we're anemic because the cells of the body have the same need for mail. That's why Margaret's heart rate was high. She was breathless after just two minutes on the treadmill because oxygen demand increases during exercise—the muscles that are being used require a higher supply of oxygen. Then the heart has to beat even faster, and in an elderly patient that can quickly lead to huge problems. The coronary arteries, the blood vessels that deliver oxygen to the heart itself, can only carry blood effectively as the heart muscle relaxes. With the faster heart rate, the heart muscle spends less time in relaxation, and soon the heart itself is starving for oxygen. If cells in the heart begin to die in the process, we call it a myocardial infarction, what laymen call a heart attack.

There's an interesting point about all of this. Remember back in Chapter Two, I talked about hemoglobin saturated with oxygen being bright red and hemoglobin that is empty-handed being dark purple? This is why people who are in oxygen debt have blue lips. The point I want to make is this: you can't get the cool cyanotic color to your skin if you don't have enough hemoglobin. So a person who is severely anemic can die of oxygen debt before he or she even gets blue lips.

Anemic Christians have a lack of grace-carriers bringing the gospel to their souls.

We've talked about the abundance of grace that's available. The limit isn't on the supply end. Just like oxygen, it seems to be in endless supply, but without a carrier, grace can't get to where we need it. That's just like a body without enough hemoglobin, the oxygen carrier.

So if the supply is abundant, where's the problem? Invariably with the receiver. Remember what the writer of Hebrews said as he quoted from the Old Testament?

> Today, if you hear his voice, do not harden your hearts.
> —Hebrews 4:7

I've often been impressed that it doesn't read, "Today, if he will speak . . ." The problem's always on our end. We've closed the graceway. We don't have enough grace-carriers. We've forgotten to breathe.

I love a good joke, always have. But I'm not going to share one with you, at least not right now. I'm going to share a stupid one, one that is so politically incorrect that if you're blonde, you can skip right on to the next page and accept my apology. I have nothing against blondes. In fact, I think we're all blonde at some level.

Have you heard the one about the dumb blonde who goes to get her hair done? She's wearing headphones, and the stylist asks her to remove them. The dumb blonde initially refuses, but after a lengthy explanation by the beautician, the blonde removes the headset. A minute later the blonde falls over dead. This puzzles the hair stylist and piques her curiosity. When she puts on the headphones, she hears a rhythmic phrase repeated over and over. "Breathe in . . . . breathe out. Breathe in . . . . breathe out."

OK, that's ridiculous. Humans, even really dumb ones, don't just forget to breathe. But spiritually that's *exactly* what we do. And it's puzzling to me.

How can we experience the refreshing, thirst-quenching waterfall of grace one day and the next day turn back to sipping from our mud puddles, tepid collections of pond water that cannot cleanse and cannot quench?

But that's exactly what humans do. Over and over. I'm a human, I ought to know. Talk about amazing. We're amazing in our ability to forget the unforgettable greatness of God's gospel of grace. So we need regular reminders, personal headphones for those of us who are dumb blondes spiritually. And we all are!

James says it this way:

> But be doers of the word, and not hearers only, deceiving yourselves. For if anyone is a hearer of the word and not a doer, he is like a man who looks intently at his natural face in a mirror. For he looks at himself and goes away and at once forgets what he was like.
>
> —James 1:22-24

So what are the carriers, the spiritual hemoglobins that we need? The Word. Fellowship. Prayer. Regular face-to-face exposure to biblical teaching. (Notice I said, "face-to-face." The radio may deliver grace, but there's no substitute for submission to Bible teaching within the context of a local church.) We need others to provide an honest mirror of our lives.

But oh, how our society exalts the lone cowboy and praises those who pull themselves up by their own bootstraps. We've been ingrained with messages of the greatness of individualism. We've come to believe that a real man never shows his weakness. "Never let 'em see you sweat" is our motto. John Wayne and the Lone Ranger were the Hollywood heroes that my father's generation idolized. I had Indiana Jones of *The Raiders of the Lost Ark* and later films. Now we have others—Jack Bauer of *24* or Clark Kent of *Smallville*. Jack Bauer breaks all the rules. He goes against every established protocol, throws aside the orders from his superiors, and enters the fray of battle outnumbered ten to one with guns blazin'! And he always wins, but not until everything looks dark. Very dark.

Now I'm not preaching a different message than we heard in the Sunday school song, "Dare to Be a Daniel." "Dare to stand alone" is a great and biblical message when we're talking about standing against a tide of ungodliness. But too many of us have embraced the dare-to-stand-alone version of stay-at-home Christianity. *Why should I be with the hypocrites when I can read my Bible in my Lazyboy?*

Because regular exposure to honest believers and biblical teachers are means of grace delivery. And it has to be regular because we're so wired to forget, so prone not to notice the logs in our own eyes. Everyone needs someone close enough and honest enough to tell us when we have bad breath because halitosis isn't something we can tell about ourselves.

Remember, manna was to be collected daily or it got old. Jesus taught us to pray for our "daily bread." That's because feeding is to take place every day. I'm not saying we have to gather in a specific building every day. What I'm emphasizing is the need for regularity in our exposure to the gospel of grace, and there's no alternative to rubbing shoulders with others who deliver it. I can't say it better than the Bible itself:

> And let us consider how to stir up one another to love and good works, not neglecting to meet together, as is the habit of some, but encouraging one another, and all the more as you see the Day drawing near.
>
> —Hebrews 10:24-25

Have you ever run into the lethargic attitude, "If salvation is God's work from start to finish, why should I witness?" Or in my case, if God is sovereign, why am I wasting my life as a missionary? Precisely because I understand that God uses regular, ordinary things like fellowship, preaching, and teaching as means of grace to accomplish his work.

By the way, my understanding of God's sovereignty in saving those he has decided to save is what motivates me to launch into a dark world and not just sit at home on the couch. It is knowing that God is in ultimate control that gives the missionary hope for success. If I didn't think that God called people from every tribe and tongue as his Word promises, discouragement, not hope, would be my daily bread. Knowing that it's *not up to us* gives us courage and hope to minister grace to those we think will never respond. And the joy is seeing God do what we thought unachievable.

Without spiritual hemoglobin to carry grace, we find ourselves anemic, breathless, and unable to perform even wimpy tasks in God's kingdom.

Just as God uses practical means of grace as the spiritual hemoglobins to carry life to an unbeliever, so he uses practical spiritual hemoglobins as grace-carriers to bring the Christian to maturity. Without them we find ourselves anemic, breathless, and unable to accomplish even wimpy tasks in God's kingdom. We're on the treadmill for just a minute or two, and we're leaning over the electronic console, pulling for air like a fish out of water.

Before I leave this discussion of practical means of grace, I want to tell you about Somali Muslims. Perhaps it will prompt you to pray (which is a means of grace that God uses to accomplish his work). I share this to illustrate how effective practical, daily exposure to teaching is, even when the teaching is wrong.

One of my Somali language teachers is a Christian convert from Islam. Growing up, he hated Saturdays. You see, for a young Somali, Saturday was a school day. Every Saturday the children were required to bring switches to their teacher. The students gathered long, slender sticks, bound them together, and gave them to the teacher who set them on prominent display in the corner.

Now this isn't a regular school. It's called dugsi, the Islamic version of capturing the hearts of children when they are young sponges, capable of absorbing teaching, even without understanding. In Somalia this is the school that takes priority over regular schooling, the reading, writing, and arithmetic that make up the three R's of American elementary education. (Whoever called them the three R's must be related to the person who quipped that the N on the side of the Nebraska football helmet stood for Nowledge.)

You start dugsi at age four and begin the daily drills to memorize the Koran. If you miss a word, the penalty is an up-close-and-personal encounter with the switches. Multiple lashes, shirt off, if you're a guy. In front of the class. An example for the rest of the children.

And the results are predictable: Many Somali children can quote the entire Koran in Arabic (which they don't understand) by age ten. *The entire book!*

Somalia breeds some of the most dedicated, fundamentalist Muslims on the planet. One look at their dugsi and you understand.

And overcoming the indoctrination to provide fertile ground for the gospel of grace is a challenge. But again, because it's God's work we have hope, even when the odds seem stacked against us.

Why bring up dugsi? I'm certainly not advocating the use of physical and mental abuses in order to indoctrinate our children. I'm only pointing out the benefits of regular exposure to teaching. And perhaps American Christians like myself can learn from the Somali example. In terms of its value, Christian parenting is huge in its role as a means of grace delivery into the life of a child.

In this chapter I've concentrated on teaching about spiritual anemia, but just as we see many different causes of anemia in clinical practice (iron deficiency, vitamin deficiencies, etc.), so there are many causes of anemia of the soul: prayer anemia, fellowship anemia, and so on. But whatever the problem, the exhortation is the same. Regular exposure to adequate grace delivery is key!

What about Margaret?

With a hemoglobin level of 5, Margaret's heart had to rush the mailmen around at twice their normal speed in order to keep up with demand. And that could have spelled heart attack, stroke, or worse.

So her doctor ordered an urgent red blood cell transfusion, the cells that contain the hemoglobin mailmen. How many of us find our souls in similar jeopardy? On the verge of spiritual stroke or heart attack, we need an urgent infusion of grace.

Over three days we transfused her to a hemoglobin level of 10 and performed a diagnostic colonoscopy. What's that? A flexible lighted video camera on a slender tube is gently glided through the lower intestine to examine the colon wall. And there in the right colon sat the cancer that had started the whole problem. Growing undetected, colon cancers will often ooze blood, shedding the mailmen needed to deliver precious oxygen mail, leading to a mail debt of sorts. I removed Margaret's cancer and sent her home five days later to rehabilitate.

The last I heard, she was back at the wellness center preparing to challenge her husband on some Rocky Mountain trails.

We are all patients in the hands of Dr. Jesus. Are we feeling the effects of grace-poor blood in our spiritual arteries? Beware: when gospel anemia is advanced, the clinical symptoms may be missed. Let Jesus look into his black bag of grace remedies. His medical skills are unparalleled, and his hands are ever so gentle as he palpates the exact problem. Soon we'll be back in health, glorying in the only thing that can bring us life: *grace!*

For Further Reflection

1. What grace-carriers bring the gospel to your soul? Why is there sometimes a lack of grace-carriers? What can you do about that?

2. What do anemic Christians look like, figuratively speaking? What's the cure?

3. "We need others to provide an honest mirror of our lives." Why? How can others help you see your own need more clearly? Why can't we be Lone Rangers spiritually?

4. If salvation is God's work, and not yours, why should you witness to others? Put differently, does the sovereignty of God mean you don't need to try to win others to Christ?

5. What is the value of teaching your children and others daily? Do you agree that this is valuable even when the teaching is wrong?

CHAPTER TEN

Mouth-to-Mouth Resuscitation:

Exhaling Grace

remember the first time I gave mouth-to-mouth resuscitation. It was back when I was a medical student, before those cute little pocket masks that keep your lips from actually touching the patient came into vogue. I was on the medicine service when I heard the overhead intercom sounding a "code blue" and the location. I was close by and was the first one into the room besides the nurse who had sent for help.

The patient was an older female. I knew what had to be done. I quickly assessed her respirations. Nothing. Time to give a few quick breaths and check a pulse. I pinched her nose between my thumb and index finger and tilted her head back to open the airway. Then I sealed my lips against hers and blew. Her chest rose. I removed my lips. Her breath rushed back out. I checked a pulse. Again nothing. I started chest compressions and started cycling through compressions and respirations until the code team of residents arrived.

Did you ever wonder why what you breathe out could save someone's life?

Why does that work? I thought we breathed in oxygen and breathed out carbon dioxide. Well, that's true, but only partially. You see, the air we're breathing at sea level is 21 percent oxygen. What we breathe out is 16 percent oxygen, in addition to carbon dioxide and other gases.

That's why it works. The oxygen debt in the dying patient is so profound that oxygen at almost any level is beneficial.

I suppose it goes without saying that the only way to breathe out oxygen is to breathe in oxygen. And we cannot breathe out grace unless we breathe in grace.

It's an interesting extension of the metaphor to realize that with the great amount of oxygen available in our atmosphere, we only use up a small fraction of what we take in. And, no wonder of wonders, we use only a minute portion of the grace that we're exposed to as well.

I don't cry. OK, that's not entirely true, but I am rarely touched so deeply that I shed a tear. Perhaps that's a societal problem, as we prefer our men to be strong and silent, although we're seeing a small change in recent years as men are now encouraged to get in touch with their emotions. It may also be a result of years spent in and around human tragedy. The surgeon needs to steel himself or herself against emotional attachments in order to make the right decisions. At least that's what I was taught. And part of that is true. But in another way, that is baloney.

There are few things more powerful in a healing relationship than a healer who owns the pain of the patient.

I brought this up because I cried the other day. I was watching a DVD. No, it wasn't a Hollywood manipulation of my emotions. It was a true documentary, the story of New Tribes missionaries Mark and Gloria Zouk. The Mouk tribe resides in remote Papua New Guinea and lived an existence of superstition and fear. That is, until the Zouks moved in to master their culture and language and eventually shared the good news of the gospel of grace.

After months of study, Mark began teaching through the Bible, telling stories chronologically. The entire tribe attended the sessions. No one wanted to miss it, not even the sick or pregnant women who were in labor. He told the stories of Adam and Eve, of God's providing a substitute lamb for Abraham just when he was about to sacrifice his son Isaac, and of the exodus of the children of Israel during the first Passover. After weeks of preparation, he introduced the story of Jesus, culminating in the crucifixion as Christ became the substitute lamb to die for our sins.

What was so amazing is that the entire tribe stood up and confessed their belief in Christ. Then in a spontaneous celebration of joy at knowing their sins had been forgiven, they began to jump together. The entire tribe yelled for joy, hugging and jumping in an explosion of rejoicing that went on for two hours!

It was the expression of joy by the Mouk people that brought tears to my eyes and thickened my voice. "Ee-Taow!" they shouted. "Ee-Taow!" This means, "It is true!"

Even as the rejoicing continued, Mark began to plan his next step—helping the young believers share their newfound faith. A comment on the DVD stood out to me as a sad commentary of much of today's church. As he watched the Mouk people dancing with joy, Mark couldn't imagine explaining to them that many Christians never share their faith.

How can anyone who has been given such great news *not* share it? It would be like breathing in and never exhaling.

I saw the explosion of happiness in the Mouk tribe at being forgiven. How could anyone not share such wonderful news? Not to share the fantastic news of the gospel would simply not compute.

So why does it compute with us? Are we blinded to our own wretchedness? Are we unmoved by the promise of eternal glory? Do we not realize that we were on our way to hell, a fate we certainly deserved? What flimsy excuses we use to justify our silence.

They'll think I'm a fanatic.

What if they ask me a question and I don't know the answer?

I can't open my mouth. I just laughed at an off-color joke.

I can't force my opinions on others. Everyone has a right to his or her own opinion.

God's going to save whom he's going to save, no matter what I do, right?

Can you see the gospel debt in our response?

Invariably, we hold our tongues because we are, at least at that moment, living out of a false gospel. The message of the false gospel of pride is that my reputation is at stake. What others think of me is the important thing. I can't share my faith because I might look bad. I want others to treasure me.

The true message of the gospel is one that gives Christ all the glory. The work was only his. He is the one we treasure, and our delight is in his reputation, not in ours. Our joy is wrapped up in seeing Christ become the treasure that he is in as many hearts as possible.

So we find ourselves in gospel debt, this time hopelessly trying to make up for our insufficient view of the cross and the work of God's grace by an attitude that says, "I'm not that bad. I want others to think well of me."

Sometimes I need a cold slap in the face. I need to remind myself of reality: Christ died to save sinners, and nothing, certainly not my reputation, is more important than bringing that news to thirsty souls.

What the world needs is grace.

They just don't know it or see it.

So should I force the gospel message on everyone I see? Only if you want to be operating out of another false gospel, trying to make up for gospel debt.

I can imagine you thinking, I just thought you said that NOT sharing the gospel meant I was operating out of gospel debt. Now you're saying that sharing the gospel is wrong too?

Yes, when it's done out of a debtor's work ethic.

Grace needs to be shared out of the overflow of a heart in love with the Savior, not out of the I-should'ves. You know what that is. I should've done this. I should've done that.

Let's look at this positively. What should it look like? Grace respiration—grace regularly taken in and naturally flowing out—is a consequence of a life that finds its boast in the cross. Remember the diagram we described in Chapter Three? When we are walking in the reality that the cross is completely sufficient to place us in right standing with a perfect God, grace flows from us as naturally as exhaling oxygen.

A life saturated in grace is a life characterized by prizing Christ above all competition. When we live with Christ as our hope (and not ourselves, our investment portfolio, our successful children, our house or possessions, or even our successful ministries in the church), something extraordinary happens. Actually it's sad that I need to describe it in those terms. It's only extraordinary because it's rare. So few of us are living grace-filled lives that what is supposed to be natural respiration seems remarkable.

When physicians chart their patient's progress, they note the respiratory rate and describe the respiratory sounds and effort, but they don't simply say, "Breathing in and out." Why? Because:

Breathing defines life.

In the same way, grace respiration is a *natural* characteristic of the Christian life. At least it should be. Grace in. Grace out. In keeping with our respiratory metaphor, ask yourself why we breathe out oxygen. Because as long as we breathe in oxygen, we cannot *not* breathe out oxygen. Because oxygen is in abundant supply and our bodies cannot possibly use it all up, we naturally breathe it out. We simply cannot not do it.

As long as we are alive, it is not possible to *not* breathe out oxygen.

Likewise, I believe that as long as our life is being saturated by grace, it will be impossible not to breathe it out to those around us.

Paul says it like this:

> But thanks be to God, who in Christ always leads us in triumphal procession, and through us spreads the fragrance of the knowledge of him everywhere. For we are the aroma of Christ to God among those who are being saved and among those who are perishing.
>
> —2 Corinthians 2:14-15

I'm "the aroma of Christ"? A sweet "fragrance"? Or am I the self-righteous stench of someone enthralled with myself?

When is the last time someone asked you why you're different? "Why do you have hope?" If you are living a life of grace, with Christ as your treasure, that will happen because you will be different. Peaceful. Joyful in spite of life's difficulties. Living life with a unique focus. The cross of Christ, and not your latest hobby, will be your single passion.[13]

> . . . but in your hearts regard Christ the Lord as holy, always being prepared to make a defense to anyone who asks you for a reason for the hope that is in you.
>
> —1 Peter 3:15

Perhaps they don't ask because our lives don't look any different from anyone else's.[14] If this is your experience, I'd encourage you to spend some time with the ABC's of resuscitation. When we spend time allowing grace to circulate in our lives, we are changed, and the overflow of that grace to others is a by-product.

If we're living our lives in gospel debt, we won't see grace overflowing to others around us. Conversely, when the graceway is open to allow grace in, grace flowing out will come as an expected consequence.

Jesus warned us about this in a direct way, so as to remove any doubt about the importance of exhaling grace.

> For what does it profit a man to gain the whole world and forfeit his life? For what can a man give in return for his life? For whoever is ashamed of me and of my words in this adulterous and sinful generation, of him will the Son of Man also be ashamed when he comes in the glory of his Father with the holy angels.
>
> —Mark 8:36-38

Ouch. If we are ever tempted to enhance our reputation by not sharing the gospel, let's return to the ABC's because we're certainly in the throes of gospel debt!

Before I tie this chapter up, I want you to think again about breathing. When you take a deep breath, only the oxygen that gets down into the microscopic air sacs does you any good because that's where the oxygen has contact with the bloodstream. The oxygen that only flows into the windpipe doesn't contribute to getting oxygen into the blood where it is needed. We call the breathing of air in and out of the trachea, or windpipe, dead-space ventilation because it doesn't contribute to the process of oxygenating your blood.

Stay with me. There's a point to all of this. Remember that the oxygen you breathe out can save another person's life during mouth-to-mouth resuscitation. But who benefits first from the oxygen you breath out?

You do. Think about it. You exhale a mixture of gas that contains carbon dioxide and oxygen. But you can't completely empty your trachea of exhaled gas, so that will be the first air that flows back into your lungs with your next breath. So the first one to benefit from the oxygen you exhale is yourself!

My point is this: when you are exhaling grace to those around you, don't forget to include yourself. How many of us find it difficult to show ourselves grace? For many of us who fight with perfectionism, this may be particularly hard. Perhaps you wallow in guilty feelings, condemning yourself and behaving in a way toward yourself that you'd never behave toward others.

Grace respiration means that you should be the first recipient of the grace exhaled into the world.

The command of the Torah, often repeated in the New Testament, is plain but misunderstood.

> . . . you shall love your neighbor as yourself.
> —Leviticus 19:18b

That's self-explanatory, right? But the part of the command we ignore is what the command hinges on. We have to love ourselves in order to love others. Remember, as long as we're holding up the measuring sticks in judgment of our own lives, we are holding it up in evaluation of others.[15] And that's a grace-killer.

Somehow we've grown up with the pious, self-effacing notion that it's wrong to love ourselves. But if God loves us, we only spite his judgment if we feel unworthy. We've come to think that humility means we think we're no good. But who are we to call unworthy what he calls holy? And that's what we are: his righteousness.

I know I've concentrated a lot on the depth of our sin, but remember that the work of the cross to bridge the gap between our sinfulness and his holiness accomplished a fantastic switch. Christ's record has become my record. So yes, now I am holy, lovable, and worthy of grace—in Christ.

My prayer is that you will become so grace-saturated that you become a channel to resuscitate a dying world around you.

And don't forget to show yourself a little grace in the process, okay?

I guess I should tell you about that first patient I performed mouth-to-mouth resuscitation on. I'd like to be able to say that I helped bring her back. It would be a grand medical-save story.

But that's not what happened. She died. The resident team worked hard for twenty minutes, going through all the resuscitation drugs, pumping on her chest, the whole deal. But she died anyway.

I guess that makes another point about grace delivery though. Our job, our calling, is to carry the fragrance of grace into a thirsty world. But ultimately it's up to God whether the recipients find life or not.

The world is dying without grace. And some of them will find life through us. Let's get out there and exhale grace!

For Further Reflection

1. "The only way to breathe out oxygen is to breathe in oxygen. And we cannot breathe out grace unless we breathe in grace." What does this mean for your spiritual life? How can you breathe in grace?

2. How is it possible for people who have been forgiven for so much and have been given such great good news to sometimes not share it?

3. Who is your greatest delight—yourself or Jesus? How can you tell? How can you get yourself out of the way and give the Savior the prominence he deserves?

4. "Grace respiration—grace regularly taken in and naturally flowing out—is a consequence of a life that finds its boast in the cross." What does it mean to boast in the cross? What does this have to do with breathing grace?

5. How do you benefit from breathing out grace to others? Is it selfish to think this way? What does this show you about God?

CHAPTER ELEVEN

Fake Breathing

ew things are more impressive to a surgeon than a sucking chest wound. Even the name carries a sort of grossness to it. A sucking chest wound is just what it sounds like: a hole is opened up through the chest cavity (rib cage) so that as the victim (uh, patient) tries to breathe, air sucks in and out through the defect, rushing back and forth, usually with a moist whistling noise and a spray of blood.

Fortunately, these injuries are rare in civilian hospitals. It's seen more commonly with impaling injuries or close-range shotgun blasts that leave large skin defects as they penetrate.

The problem is this: the larger the defect, the more air will rush in and out of the sucking chest wound and less and less through the windpipe into the lungs where it can be used to transport oxygen into the blood.

The reason is mechanical. Air will always follow the path of least resistance. A healthy individual lowers the pressure in the chest by forcing down the diaphragm muscle and lifting the ribcage outward. As a result of the lower pressure in the chest, air rushes into the nose or mouth, down the trachea, and into the air sacs for gas exchange. Not so if the patient has an open wound in the chest. If the wound in the chest is two-thirds of the diameter of the trachea, air will preferentially rush in and out of the open chest wound and not in and out of the mouth and lungs where it is needed.

This results in a rather dramatic presentation. The person is working hard at breathing, but air doesn't flow into the mouth. On examination the chest rises and falls. It looks like breathing, but it's not. This is deadly.

And fast. The only oxygen being pulled into the chest cavity is not inside the lung where it is needed. It is outside the lung.

So it's what I call fake breathing. Actually any air movement in and out of the patient that doesn't contribute to actually getting oxygen into the blood is known as dead-space ventilation.

In a sucking chest wound, this type of ventilation is aptly named dead-space: the person will suffocate and die, even though the chest is vigorously involved in muscle activity that looks like breathing.

The first priority is always airway. In a patient with an open chest wound, the airway is open, but physiological breathing isn't able to occur. So the first order of business becomes sealing the wound. That way, when the patient tries to inhale, air will flow through the mouth and into the lungs again.

The treatment is simple. And lifesaving.

If only fake gospel respiration was as easy to treat!

There is a serious pathology infecting the church, squeezing grace out of the gospel and substituting something that looks a lot like grace respiration on the surface. But it's death to the church and individual alike. It's the spiritual equivalent of a sucking chest wound. There's a lot of breathing activity but no life.

The malady is sometimes so insidious that even the person infected can't recognize it. It's simply a works-gospel, where the attention is subtly shifted from the giver to the gifts, from working out of gratitude to working out of debt, and from right motives to working for recognition.

We slip from working in a ministry that exalts the name of Christ to exalting the name of the ministry.

We preach to the itching ears of man and not to souls thirsty for grace.

We focus on working for God rather than on God.

We worship to be seen by men.

We speak up in Sunday school not to encourage but to impress.

We attend a spiritual gathering to be seen, not to see God.

We are OK making an anonymous gift as long as someone sees us putting it in the offering.

We underline our Bible not because our souls are in gospel debt but because we want our spouses to notice.

Have you ever said, "I'll pray for you," just to be nice? What was your motive? Did you mean it, or did you want to look spiritual?

Have you ever done something good, even religious, simply because your reputation depended upon it?

All of these things look like manifestations of the gospel of grace, but God knows our hearts.

Jesus was never one to mince words, was he? Look at how he handled the Pharisees:

> You blind guides, straining out a gnat and swallowing
> a camel. Woe to you, scribes and Pharisees, hypocrites!

> For you clean the outside of the cup and the plate, but
> inside they are full of greed and self-indulgence. You blind
> Pharisee! First clean the inside of the cup and the plate,
> that the outside also may be clean. Woe to you, scribes
> and Pharisees, hypocrites! For you are like whitewashed
> tombs, which outwardly appear beautiful, but within are
> full of dead people's bones and all uncleanness. So you also
> outwardly appear righteous to others, but within you are
> full of hypocrisy and lawlessness.
>
> —Matthew 23:24-28

Some of us don't fall prey to doing good works just to look good to others, but our good works are infected by another common virus: the hope that God will find us just a bit more acceptable if we do something good. The news of the gospel that there's nothing we can do to make him love us less and nothing we can do to make him love us more is something many of us assent to in our minds but not in our hearts.

Some people harbor unspoken fears that their particular set of sins is beyond the reaches of grace. Others feel that God will forgive but that he expects an appropriate amount of guilt feelings before he's approachable.

My pastor back in Virginia, Phil Smuland, liked to put it this way: there isn't a sin you can confess that isn't already forgiven. That knowledge is what brings the power to change, which is the essence of repentance. Otherwise repentance becomes penitence.

It all comes down to motive, doesn't it?

The gospel of grace is all about the get-to's. A works-gospel is all about the have-to's or ought-to's.

Why worship? We get to.

Why sacrifice, work, give, bless, teach, visit, love, encourage, and comfort? We get to.

There is no greater privilege than being the body of Christ to reach a hurting world. The honor of being his fingers is a get-to. And the phenomenal part of the deal is that we trust, he works through us, and then he rewards us in the end for letting him use us. That's a win-win.

In a works-gospel of fake breathing, we have to.

Now I know that there are occasions when we are feeling anything but the privilege of getting to, and yet we have an obligation to move forward. Have you ever agreed to do something good in advance, and then when the time came, you felt none of the emotion that you needed to carry on? Preachers sometimes feel this. Teachers occasionally feel this. Sunday morning is here, and you have to preach, and you feel like staying at home in the recliner. But you preach anyway. You have to.

I know we won't always have the get-to, glad emotions prompting us to serve. But during those times when we press on in spite of our feelings, we are operating by faith in God's provision, not in our own strength, and so by definition we are operating in grace and not in gospel debt.

Those times aren't the have-to's that I'm talking about. I'm talking about working because you want the reward and recognition. That's operating out of the false gospel of pride (*treasure me!*). The other popular, yet very detrimental have-to is working out of a debtor mentality. That's when we're operating in the false gospel I call grace-plus or cross-plus.

Grace-plus is when we mentally assent to our standing as sons and daughters by grace, but we think we're more acceptable if we do something good. That's grace-plus.

Or we know Christ paid our sin-debt on Calvary, but we think we need to spend a few hours crying or a few months feeling guilty too. That's cross-plus, a false gospel.

When I was a teenager, just a baby in my Christian faith, I was concerned that I needed to confess every sin each night before I went to bed. It was a bit of a compulsive naming of every type of offense. I figured I really couldn't name all my individual sins, but I could at least hit the main categories. So I began my nightly routine, "Forgive me for any thought, desire, imagination, or fantasy that I've had or done that wasn't pleasing to you." I felt I had to name them to be forgiven. That's cross-plus, a false gospel!

Read closely. I'm not saying confession of sin is wrong. It is very right. But if confession is needed on top of the work of the cross to purchase our forgiveness, then confession has become a works-gospel.

Confession is a necessary part of assenting to the truth that we need God, that we have failed. Confession is what opens the graceway. If we don't see our sin, we don't acknowledge our need, and so we remain in gospel debt.

What was happening to me as a teen was that I was using confession in the wrong way—not as a way of mentally assenting to my need for grace, an act that restores my fellowship with God, but as an accounting necessary to cleanse my record.

I'll bet that some of you who are trapped in this subtle works-gospel are already starting to protest, "What about 1 John 1:9?" OK, let's look at the passage in context.

> If we say we have fellowship with him while we walk in darkness, we lie and do not practice the truth. But if we walk in the light, as he is in the light, we have fellowship with one another, and the blood of Jesus his Son cleanses us from all sin. If we say we have no sin, we deceive ourselves, and the truth is not in us. If we confess our sins, he is faithful and just to forgive us our sins and to cleanse us from all unrighteousness.
>
> —1 John 1:6-9

"If we confess our sins, he is faithful . . . to forgive us our sins" comes within the context of a series of if . . . then statements.

> If we say we have fellowship with him while we walk in darkness, we lie . . . (v. 6)

If we walk in the light . . . we have fellowship . . . and the blood of Jesus . . . cleanses us from all sin. (v. 7)

If we say we have no sin . . . the truth is not in us. (v. 8)

If we confess our sins, he is faithful . . . to forgive us our sins. (v. 9)

Taken within the context of the entire New Testament, we would hardly be able to argue that verse 7 teaches that we have to walk in the light in order for the blood of Jesus to cleanse us from sin. That would be a definite works-gospel. We understand this verse to affirm that walking in the light is part-and-parcel of the Christian life, a life where the blood of Christ cleanses us from all sins.

Likewise, verse 9 teaches us that he is faithful and just to forgive our sins if we confess (because seeing our sin-need is necessary or we won't come to the cross for the solution), but it doesn't say that if we don't confess, we'll be damned.

The context of the passage is fellowship with other believers and fellowship with the Father. Confession allows recognition of our need and restoration of fellowship (communication and communion), but it doesn't purchase our salvation.

When Jesus died on the cross, he was the perfect sacrifice to place us in right standing before his Father. The cross is the supreme manifestation of grace. It is the expansion of our understanding of the cross that keeps us out of gospel debt. When he died, he paid the price for all our sins—past, present, and future. To add one condition, even the confession of sin, as a requirement for payment of our debt is a slap in the face of God's provision, a spite to the grace of God.

> But when Christ had offered for all time a single sacrifice for sins, he sat down at the right hand of God, waiting from that time until his enemies should be made a footstool for his feet.
>
> —Hebrews 10:12-13

Cross-plus gospel is a flat denial of grace, a slap in the face of our generous God.

Sometimes surgeons can be crass in their bantering, something we need to watch in order not to offend a patient. When we are out of the earshot of the patients, it would not be unusual to hear one of my partners say, "It's time to look under the hood."

What does that mean?

It's an automotive metaphor. It may sound a bit crude, but it's not meant that way. The statement only means that it's time to operate, to open the patient up to see what is going on and fix the problem.

Surgeons have another saying: "Don't let the skin stand between you and a diagnosis." All that means is, don't be reluctant to explore a patient (to do surgery) if you need to find out what's going on.

Things may look right on the surface, even when cancers are eating away the patient on the inside. Sometimes it takes a scalpel to provide the answer.

I say this only to point out that a works-gospel can look exactly like the gospel of grace on the surface. It might take a spiritual scalpel of sorts to dissect and diagnose the motive.

Scalpels like that belong in the hands of the wise, usually the Great Physician himself.

> For the LORD sees not as man sees: man looks on the outward appearance, but the LORD looks on the heart.
>
> —1 Samuel 16:7b

This chapter is not meant to prompt a critical investigation of our brothers' and sisters' fruit. That would certainly be an act of graceless gospel debt! I only want us to think about how easy it is to slip into fake breathing, giving grace for the wrong reasons, and to prompt us quickly to reaffirm our need of grace (*A* is for *acknowledge* . . .).

≡ **In an open chest wound oxygen follows the path of least resistance and results in fake breathing.**

≡ **In our spiritual lives we often default to the path of least resistance. In a moment's time we're working for reward, having stumbled headlong into a fake gospel.**

Remember, in a sucking chest wound the air/oxygen always follows the path of least resistance, through the wound and not into the mouth and lungs. Spiritually we seem to be wired the same way. Sometimes the path of least resistance is works. It just seems to make natural sense to us that if we do good things, God will like us more. So our natural default, the path of least resistance, is to fall headlong into a works mentality. We do it almost as easily as we breathe.

It's very possible to start in grace and finish in gospel debt.

Perhaps the good news of the gospel of grace is too good for the mind of natural man. It is almost inconceivable that God could be so full of grace toward undeserving scum. Perhaps one reason that Islam is spreading in the world is that it appeals to our own seemingly innate desire to do it ourselves.[16] We want to be in control. The driver's seat, not the passenger's, is the place for us. So a false religion holding up the scales of good and evil to determine our fate makes sense. We get to be in control.

But that's not the gospel of grace! If there was one thing that got the apostle Paul fired up, it was a gospel that was something other than grace alone, faith alone, and Christ alone.

> Are you so foolish? Having begun by the Spirit, are you now being perfected by the flesh?
>
> —Galatians 3:3b

We're saved by grace, and we need to walk by grace. Every step.

But I stumble all the time. God can't be happy about that. He has to be angry with me.

Angry, yes. But not at you. At your sin. That's an important distinc-
tion.[17] It may seem like semantics, but it isn't. It drives straight to the
heart of the gospel of grace.

I don't know how many church services I've sat through where the
sermon can be summed up like this: "_____ more." I left it blank for
you to fill in. Pray more. Fast more. Study your Bible more. Witness
more. Worship more. Give more.

You get the picture. And most of the time the preacher said it with
a note of grace, I'm sure. But given our goal-oriented, accomplish-
something-for-Christ-today bend, Christians tend to come out of
sermons like this with a sort of heaviness, an overhanging cloud
of obligation. The clouds are pregnant with have-to rain, and the
horizon is dark.

Because it is so easy to default to a works-gospel, we have to dig in
on this issue and make a stand. Learn to recognize graceless religion
in your life, and use every weapon at your disposal to fight it.

> For freedom Christ has set us free; stand firm therefore,
> and do not submit again to a yoke of slavery.
>
> —Galatians 5:1

Submission is passive. Slipping back into fake breathing is passive.
Paul says, "Stand firm" and "*do not* submit." I love his metaphor: "yoke
of slavery." If you've ever seen one of these, you'll know in an instant
that you don't want to go there. Fight for this, my brothers and sisters.
This is of grave importance!

Fake breathing is deadly. A life is at stake.

Fake gospel is worse. Eternity is at stake.

Listen to the immediacy in Paul's urging:

> I am astonished that you are so quickly deserting him
> who called you in the grace of Christ and are turning to a
> different gospel—not that there is another one, but there
> are some who trouble you and want to distort the gospel
> of Christ. But even if we or an angel from heaven should

preach to you a gospel contrary to the one we preached to you, let him be accursed. As we have said before, so now I say again: If anyone is preaching to you a gospel contrary to the one you received, let him be accursed.

—Galatians 1:6-9

Before I close this chapter, I want you to know one more thing about sucking chest wounds. The patient is in the throes of oxygen debt, making physical movements that look like breathing, though no respiration is occurring, right? The truth is, their breathing efforts don't look normal. Yes, it looks like breathing, but more exactly, it looks like labored breathing. The patient is fighting for air. Desperate! Panting, puffing, and getting nowhere!

I know I said that a works-gospel is sometimes hard to distinguish from the real thing, but there may be clues that we're slipping into trouble. Are we striving for grace? Desperate, panting or puffing, and getting nowhere?

Maybe, just maybe we've slipped into fake breathing and we need to take another look at treatment.

For Further Reflection

1. How is a works gospel different from the gospel of grace? What is the focus in each? Is it possible to move from truth to self-centeredness without realizing it's happening? How can you avoid this?

2. Do you agree there is no sin you can confess that isn't already forgiven?

3. How are a grace-plus gospel and a cross-plus gospel alike? How are they different? What is the error of each? The danger?

4. How does fake breathing sometimes become part of your spiritual life? With what consequences?

5. Do you agree that when you sin, God is not angry at you but at your sin? What does this really mean? How does this encourage you in your walk with God?

CHAPTER TWELVE

Spiritual Sepsis

*S*itting here with my laptop, I find myself in gospel debt, wishing this next story was about me—my cool accomplishment in saving a newborn baby.

But it's not. So I'll have to believe the gospel promise that not only is salvation God's work, but so is the rest of the universe. It's all about him, his glory, and the fact that Christ's sacrifice is sufficient to put me in right standing with God. So I don't need to worry about looking good or better than I am.

This true story isn't about me. But it's so cool I wish it was. It's about a baby's first breath, the very first exposure to life-giving oxygen.

From the first moment of life to our last heartbeat, breathing defines life. Think about it—the very first thing an obstetrician does during a delivery, even before the baby's body is out, is clear the airway. As soon as the head is out, a small rubber suction ball with a soft pointed tip is squeezed and inserted into the baby's mouth and nose to suction out any secretions. That way when the baby takes his or her first breath, in preparation for that initial scream, he or she won't suck in a bunch of mucous . . . or worse.

Most of the time everything goes smoothly. But prepared obstetricians look for a rattlesnake in every gulch, to lessen the chances of being bitten. One of those rattlesnakes is called meconium.

Excuse me? What's that?

Meconium is the medical name given to a baby's first bowel movement. It's usually soft and greenish and doesn't have bacteria like adult stools. Usually a baby has its first bowel movement after delivery, but occasionally, especially if the baby is late in coming, it might have its first bowel movement inside the uterus, right out into the amniotic fluid that the baby swims in.

And that spells trouble. As long as the meconium stays out of the respiratory tract, everything is fine, but the key is preventing the newborn from taking a breath before any meconium can be suctioned out of the baby's mouth. The whole point is to prevent aspiration of the meconium (the entry of meconium into the lungs) when the baby pulls hard for its first breath. If that happens, the baby's airway is blocked, respiratory distress occurs, and the baby faces the downward spiral of pneumonia and sometimes death.

Fortunately, as I've indicated, most of this is preventable with the proper suction equipment to clear the baby's airway during delivery.

Which brings me to my cool story.

When I was in medical school at Medical College of Virginia, a fellow M-3 (third-year medical student) was in the elevator on his way to the labor and delivery suite with a woman in labor. In general, an elevator is the worst place to be in an emergency. There are virtually no supplies. And there's nowhere to run if you need help. And if you're in a medical emergency and you lift the phone, all you're going to get is a security guard.

Well, you guessed it. This baby wasn't in the mood for hanging out in his comfortable uterine home any longer. So the medical student delivered the baby in the elevator. But to make matters worse, there was meconium in the amniotic fluid.

But my classmate didn't have a nifty red suction apparatus.

So he did what hundreds of missionary doctors in developing countries do every day: he improvised.

He pulled a nineteen-cent Bic pen from his white coat and discarded the central ink compartment, leaving the hard plastic tube. Bingo—a suction tube! And then (you can stop reading if you're skittish about gross medical stories—just pick it up in the next section) he sucked out the baby's mouth with the pen-shaft.

He sucked out the meconium and saved the baby's life.

That's gross.

But it's way cool.

So far, most of the problems we've talked about have had to do with oxygen delivery, but in this chapter I want to shift attention to another problem: underutilization of available oxygen. That can be a late consequence of meconium aspiration if pneumonia sets in. The next big hurdle is called sepsis, when infections get out of hand and everything starts looking bleak.

An interesting thing happens with oxygen utilization in severe infection. It goes down! Just when the patient needs oxygen to fight the battle of sepsis, and you would think oxygen use by the cells would go up, a problem develops in microcirculation: arterial blood, which is rich in oxygen, begins to short-circuit into veins without passing by all the cells where the oxygen is needed. This results in a higher level of oxygen returning to the heart through the veins. In essence, the blood returns the oxygen to the heart *unused*.

That brings us to another spiritual pathology, a malady I've dubbed spiritual sepsis. How often we find ourselves in this condition! There is abundant available grace. We may even know we need it, so the graceway is open. We believe the gospel is true, but dullness has settled in. We want fresh grace. We go to church for fellowship, but week after week our prayers seem cold, and the messages of grace fall upon us like rain after a long drought—nothing sinks in. The dust may settle for a day, but then it's back to spiritual famine.

Grace everywhere. And no obvious grace obstruction. Yet the grace seems to flow over our souls, which remain untouched and unmoved.

All this begs the question, how can something so amazing not affect my soul with every telling?

Why do we all seem to go through seasons of dryness, insensitive to the water-whispers of God's love?

Perhaps we haven't looked hard enough for an obstruction on our end. Pride, self-deception, and self-love can be subtle, almost invisible grace-blockers.

Or perhaps it's because for a season God has decided, in his love, to test us with silence.

Spiritual sepsis results in famine in the midst of rain. Our souls are crusty, unreceptive to gentle showers of grace.

Let's consider sepsis scenario number one: the problem is on our end. We are in a grace-saturated environment, yet our souls are unreceptive. The grace seems to run off our souls without leaving a nourishing mark.

The problem may be twofold here.

Sometimes heart-ground needs preparation before hearing the Word.

> Sow for yourselves righteousness;
> reap steadfast love;

> break up your fallow ground,
> for it is the time to seek the LORD,
> that he may come and rain righteousness upon you.
>
> —Hosea 10:12

Why prepare the ground? Because it's time to seek the Lord. Without plowing, seed goes to waste. Without the softening effect of prayer and repentance, God's word of grace runs off unused.

What do you do if you're in a noisy, crowded room and you hear someone talking about you? If you're curious, you may walk closer, or you might just direct sneak your finger up behind one ear and push it forward to catch more of the sound.

> Incline your ear, and hear the words of the wise,
> and apply your heart to my knowledge.
>
> —Proverbs 22:17

What is the proper soul-posture for receiving grace?

You see, there's a proper posture for listening. Facing the sound. Ears pushed forward. All attention on the source. How many of us parents have tried to get the attention of a child whose focus isn't on us? "Sit up straight and listen!"

And there is a proper soul-posture for receiving grace. Unfortunately, preparation is often overlooked.

I've never seen a published survey, but I suspect one of the most common times for family arguments is on the way to church on Sunday. The kids are upset because it's the weekend, they stayed up late, and they wanted to sleep in. One or both parents are frustrated at being late. A teenager is still dressing in the car. Another younger sibling forgot his shoes altogether. One spouse criticizes the other for breaking the speed limit.

And on and on and on.

We arrive for worship warmed not by anticipation of God's presence but by our emotions that have been steamed by family friction.

No wonder we sit under words of grace and they don't sink in. The message never had a chance to penetrate our fallow ground.

My suggestion? Begin preparation by doing what you can on Saturday night. Set bedtimes for children. And pray. Spend time asking God to open your heart to his Word, his truth, and his grace.

The proper soul-posture? Prepared. Watered. That means you don't shut off the water hose of grace by pride. Then the seed of God's Word can have a chance to bear fruit.

And oh yes, quickly acknowledge your need of grace instead of being defensive when your spouse points out that you are speeding!

The second problem with lack of receptivity to grace is closely related to the first. Grace is choked out by the cares, concerns, and anxieties of life. Our attention is so much on our problems that we can't see the grace that's all around us.

Try something right now. Pick out an object in the room where you are sitting, preferably an item much bigger than your thumb. Then hold up your right thumb at arm's length, still looking at the item. Because your thumb is much smaller than the object, you can still see the object, right? Now close one eye, and slowly bring your thumb toward your eye. Eventually the object disappears, and all you see is your thumb.

You could hide the Empire State building behind your thumb if your hand is close enough to your face.

It's all a matter of perspective.

If the devil has ABC's of drying up the Christian life, *A* is for *anxiety*.

Anxieties and cares can hide the grace of God. In proper perspective, they are miniscule compared to the riches of God's grace. The problem is that our focus is on our worries. In effect, we've pulled the anxiety so close to our eyes that everything else is blocked out, including God.

In the parable of the sower, Jesus described unreceptive ground:

> As for what was sown among thorns, this is the one who hears the word, but the cares of the world and the deceitfulness of riches choke the word, and it proves unfruitful.
>
> —Matthew 13:22

I believe this parable is referring to the Word sown in the heart at salvation, but nonetheless the principle applies. Cares and riches can choke out the effect of grace by diverting our attention, inducing a kind of spiritual sepsis as a result.

> Let not your hearts be troubled. Believe in God; believe also in me.
>
> —John 14:1

I've always been intrigued by the language in that verse. "*Let not* your hearts . . . ." Yes, we have a role. We can make a choice to pray instead of worrying.

> . . . do not be anxious about anything, but in everything by prayer and supplication with thanksgiving let your requests be made known to God. And the peace of God, which surpasses all understanding, will guard your hearts and minds in Christ Jesus.
>
> —Philippians 4:6-7

Of course, our own insensitivity to grace makes the state of our nation all the more understandable. Never in history have there been so many churches, so many books, and so many radio stations all proclaiming the gospel. And yet we watch as our society embraces postmodern relativism. The gospel of grace is presented to dull expressions, faces that mindlessly say, "What may be truth for you isn't truth for me."

Grace rains on us and on many around us, but it runs off unabsorbed and unused. Just like oxygen in sepsis.

We are like spiritual arteries, delivering grace to a septic world.

Our response should not be discouragement, since we are only channels in grace delivery. If it were our work, it would be time to worry.

But since it's God's work, spiritual sepsis (insensitivity to the gospel) should prompt us to pray. Ultimately, the fact that he is in control and the work doesn't depend upon us should drive us into deeper reliance on him.

In terms of ministering the gospel to a world in grace famine, prayer is huge. No, it doesn't turn the tables and make the work dependent upon our prayers. But it is a means of grace, as are fellowship and the Word. Prayer is how we align our hearts with God's and ready our hearts for his promptings so we can participate in his work.

Our prayers are a means of accomplishing the Spirit's work. Only he can convict of sin. Only he can convince a septic world of the need for new life.

If treated early with antibiotics, sepsis can be effectively interrupted and organ system failure avoided. But as with meconium aspiration, prevention is better than treatment when the patient is circling the drain.

Spiritual sepsis is better prevented as well. And that takes the penicillin of prayer.

Soften our hearts, Father, that we may respond to your grace!

For Further Reflection

1. What is spiritual sepsis? Why is it that sometimes "our souls are crusty, unreceptive to gentle showers of grace"?

2. What should be your soul's posture if you are to receive grace? What is your soul's posture today? How does it need to change?

3. How do the cares, concerns, and anxieties of life keep you from experiencing divine grace day by day? What can you do to avoid this?

4. "Let not your hearts be troubled." What is your role in not allowing worries to crowd out grace?

5. "We are like spiritual arteries, delivering grace to a septic world." How so? Are you a conduit of God's grace? Why or why not?

CHAPTER THIRTEEN

Spiritual Emboli

Being from the wrong family in a country where the men can recite their father's father's father back twenty-three generations is dangerous. Mohamed found out just how dangerous the day he was pulled from his truck, stabbed in his thigh, and left for dead on a roadside in Mogadishu, Somalia.

He pulled off his shirt, tied it around his bleeding thigh, and lay in a gutter until the next day when someone recognized him and took him to a local hospital. There a doctor explored the deep wound in Mohamed's leg and tied off his femoral artery.

That may have kept him from bleeding to death, but it created another problem. Mohamed's foot was starved of oxygen.

The doctor drew a line two inches below Mohamed's hip and told him he needed to amputate.

Mohamed refused and sought another opinion.

The second doctor wanted to test whether Mohamed's foot was still alive but lacked the sophistication or knowledge to figure it out. When he held a cigarette lighter flame up to Mohamed's ankle, Mohamed screamed in pain. *Good sign*, the doctor thought, but he wanted to be sure.

So the doctor snipped the skin off the tip of Mohamed's toe. The wound bled, and Mohamed screamed again. *Hmmm. The foot seems alive.*

For those of you reading this from the relative comfort of America, count your blessings that we have a health-care system to protect our families from treatment like that.

Mohamed crossed the Kenyan border and came to Kijabe, Kenya in search of help. His foot may have been alive, but now it was wounded, burned, and in constant pain.

I saw the patient three weeks after his injury. A few days later, we did a bypass surgery to restore blood flow to Mohamed's starving foot.

One injured leg changed Mohamed's focus. It mattered little that he had two good arms, a heart, a brain, and another good leg. The only thing that mattered was his painful foot!

Acute arterial occlusions can occur in cases like Mohamed's, when the artery is severed in an attack, or sometimes a blockage can come from inside the body in the form of an embolus.

An embolus is commonly a blood clot that forms somewhere else in the body, usually in the heart, and then breaks loose, sending the clot into the blood vessels where it lodges in an artery somewhere downstream. That's when the trouble starts. Blood can't get past the clot to deliver oxygen to the tissues further down. And that's what causes pain, the constant message that proclaims, "Send more blood."

The problem in the case of an embolus isn't the airway or the breathing or even the heart's ability to pump the oxygen around. It's that one area of the body is blocked from the life-flow of necessary oxygen.

Some of us have the spiritual equivalent of an arterial embolus. We've allowed a hurt, perhaps something originating from deep within us (like the heart in the case of emboli), to block off an area of our souls from grace. Most likely it wasn't a conscious decision not to be touched by God's love but an effort to avoid further hurt.

The problem is, one graceless area affects the whole life. One hurting foot like Mohamed's changes everything. And threatens everything. Without treatment, a leg starved of oxygen begins to release proteins into the blood from dying muscle. This causes the kidneys to fail. Then the dying cells in the leg begin to release potassium until the heart begins to beat irregularly, threatening to stop altogether.

The physiological message is that we need to expose all the rooms of our souls to God's grace. We need to remove the spiritual emboli to restore the grace-source.

What causes the clots to form?

Usually a past hurt. Mistreatment. A failed relationship. Gossip. Lost love. Rejection. A million possible offenses that lead down the same road. *I'm never going to let myself get hurt like that again!*

The only problem is that when we shut ourselves off from hurt, we shut ourselves off from grace. We allow a hurt that originates in our hearts to staunch the flow of grace to some area of our life. And in turn we have a soul shutdown. Nothing seems as bright and crisp as before. We're wearing a filter to protect our souls, but everything seems dull.

In *The Four Loves,* C. S. Lewis observes:

There is no safe investment. To love at all is to be vulnerable. Love anything and your heart will certainly be wrung and possibly be broken. If you want to make sure of keeping it intact, you must give your heart to no one, not even to an animal. Wrap it carefully round with hobbies and little luxuries; avoid all entanglements; lock it up safe in the casket or coffin of your selfishness. But in that casket—it will change. It will not be broken; it will become unbreakable, impenetrable, irredeemable. . . . The only place outside Heaven where you can be perfectly safe from all the dangers and perturbations of love is Hell.[18]

For some of us, it has been a conscious decision to avoid pain, and we've unwillingly shut down.

We created a safe room in the soul, a place of no pain—a place of graceless security.

But a graceless refuge is no real sanctuary. To experience love, we must experience the pain of potential lost love. To know forgiveness, we must forgive. The fire of bitterness may warm the heart for a season, but it will smolder as a cancer, spreading its dearth beyond its borders until it consumes us with its malignant hunger.

Bitterness is a pill we swallow but can't digest. It is regurgitated again and again until we find the grace to forgive.

> See to it that no one fails to obtain the grace of God; that no "root of bitterness" springs up and causes trouble, and by it many become defiled.
>
> —Hebrews 12:15

The writer of the New Testament book of Hebrews understood that bitterness is a natural grace-blocker. It is a sure way by which "one fails to obtain the grace of God."

But you don't know my specific circumstance. You don't know what my spouse did to me.

He knew I was interested in that property, but he bought it anyway. And he calls himself a Christian!

She betrayed my confidence. I'll never share anything with her again.

How dare he take credit for my work!

She slept with my husband!

He molested my daughter!
He laughed when I shared my problem.

Bitterness is the spiritual embolus that blocks life-giving grace.

When we apply the scalpel to the scab of bitterness, what do we find beneath the crusty covering? Pride.

Oh, great. I've been hurt, and now you're just going to tell me it's my fault, that I'm sinning.

I'm not saying the hurt was your fault. In the loving sovereignty of God, he allowed the offense to occur. Regardless of the reason, now the ball is in your court. You have a choice of responses.

Unfortunately, when I am trapped in bitterness, I've sometimes chosen a painful path. When I choose bitterness, I'm deciding, in effect, to sit on the throne. I'm in control. I get to judge. And I've decided not to forgive.

But judgment is God's job. Our job is to trust him. When we've chosen bitterness, which is default option number one for many of us, we operate within the false gospel of pride, taking a job that belongs to our loving Father. We find ourselves in gospel debt, separated from the grace and the riches of his love.

So we're hurt first by the offense and then are hurt again by the bitter embolus that keeps grace from touching our hurt. We've shot ourselves in the foot. Bitterness becomes the handgun we fondle, dreaming of our revenge. *He'll never hurt me again.* We spend time shining the barrel of our resentments, loading and unloading the gun, steeling ourselves against future hurt.

But who gets wounded in the process?

We do. The gun we designed for our protection blows a hole in our souls.

What's the way out?

Let me say from the beginning that it may be important to find a skilled Christian counselor to help you through your grief. Get over the stigma of asking for help. That's only more evidence that you're clinging to the reins when you should be trusting.

The way out begins with *acknowledging* your need. *God, I can't do this by myself. Forgive me for judging my brother. Forgive me for my pride. I need you to do this because I can't release my resentment.*

Believe the message of the gospel. You have been made righteous by the sacrifice of Christ. Your sins are gone. You are a child of God. That is the only identity that matters. You are not the judge. The work of the cross has freed you from the need to be in control or to look better than you are. What has been done to you by others is insignificant compared to the greatness of God's work in bringing you into sonship. Everything else—every act, word, or hurt—pales in the shadow of the cross. The only work that was necessary to place you in right standing with God has already been done.

Commune with God, meditating on his truths, and allow the gospel to circulate into your hurts.

And when you slip back into gospel debt and are tempted to wallow in the mud puddle of resentment, turn quickly to the fountain of grace.

Mohamed needed surgery to restore oxygen to his leg. Many of us need the spiritual scalpel of a trusted friend or pastor to help us through the forgiving process.

Sometimes a hurt looms large. It seems a mountain in our eyes.

God's grace is bigger. Remember the word from Zechariah. How is God's redemptive work accomplished in our lives? Not by our might or by our power . . .

> Then he said to me, "This is the word of the Lord to Zerubbabel: Not by might, nor by power, but by my Spirit, says the Lord of hosts. Who are you, O great mountain? Before Zerubbabel you shall become a plain. And he shall bring forward the top stone amid shouts of 'Grace, grace to it!'"
>
> —Zechariah 4:6-7

For Further Reflection

1. What types of deep hurt can keep grace from entering your soul? Without treatment, what will happen?

2. "To love at all is to be vulnerable. Love anything and your heart will certainly be wrung and possibly be broken" (C. S. Lewis). So should you play it safe and not care about anyone? Why or why not?

3. What danger does bitterness pose for your soul? What is bitterness? When you refuse to forgive, who do you believe is the judge?

4. How do the ABC's of the spiritual life (acknowledge, believe, commune with God) relate to moving past hurt and bitterness?

5. Is God's grace truly bigger than your hurt? In what ways? How does his grace bring genuine change into your heart?

CHAPTER FOURTEEN

The Great Masquerade

A rescue squad brings a comatose patient to the emergency room. The physician looks at the paramedic. "Give me the bullet."

"Twenty-two-year-old male pulled from a burning building. Blood pressure 100 systolic, heart rate 140, respirations 30 and shallow."

The physician looks over the patient. There are no apparent burns and no evidence of head trauma. The young man's face seems flushed, with no evidence of cyanosis.

Why is he unresponsive?

Drug overdose before setting a fire to cover a suicide attempt? Hmmm. A favorite Hollywood scenario, but not likely.

Diabetic coma, unable to escape on his own? Again possible, but rare. We have a saying in medicine: "When you hear hoofbeats, think horses, not zebras." This, of course, was taught to me by my professors in America and has little application to my current practice in Africa, where hoofbeats almost always mean zebras!

Knocked unconscious running from the fire? Not likely in absence of notable head trauma.

Back up and look at the history and physical.

Clue number one: pulled from a burning building.

Clue number two: face seems flushed.

The diagnosis? Carbon monoxide poisoning. A physician is trained to think of this anytime someone is in a fire, especially in a closed room. Carbon monoxide is lethal at very low doses but leaves the patient looking pink because the blood is bright red.

You see, hemoglobin molecules bind carbon monoxide molecules two hundred fifty times more tightly than they do oxygen molecules. For that reason, very small amounts of carbon monoxide quickly occupy all of the hemoglobin binding sites and leave no room for oxygen.

It's as if the mailmen decide to carry bricks and have no space left in their bags for mail. And because the patient's lips and skin don't turn blue, the patient can be dead before showing obvious signs of running out of oxygen.

There is an equally damaging philosophy masquerading as gospel truth. Some have dubbed it the prosperity gospel. Central to its teachings is the idea of health and wealth being available to every believer with enough faith and possibly a generous donation to a televangelist.

In my medical career I've been around sick people my entire adult life, and a belief system that lacks a theology of suffering is not only errant, it is damaging to the human soul afflicted with pain. As I read the New Testament, I see a God who suffered and calls us into step to follow him. I see an exaltation of the poor. I cannot help but wonder why the American church has been so easily influenced by prosperity doctrine proponents.

A look at our society may provide some answers. The U.S. spends one hundred billion dollars a year on pain-relief medications! A fraction of that could replace and run our mission hospital indefinitely.

What should I expect from a society that claims the pursuit of happiness as an inalienable right?

But pain and economic suffering are necessary parts of a fallen world. My African brothers and sisters don't seem to struggle with this as much as my American counterparts. And please don't tell them they only need to have more faith, to name it and claim it, in order to move into financial prosperity.

I heard a wise minister say, "God's will for our lives is hardly completed until the pain of staying where we are is greater than the pain of being where he wants us to be."

God has definite designs for the pain in our lives, but our orientation to get out of pain focuses us away from the messenger. We want relief—God wants our trust. He is more interested in whether we will believe in spite of the darkness than in removing the blackness around us.

But our default modus operandi is to move as soon as we feel heat. Sometimes it pays to stay put and ask what God is doing rather than run to the medicine cabinet.

Surgeons know that pain is an important message. It is irritating to be called to see a patient in the emergency room for evaluation of abdominal pain only to find that the patient has been snowed with morphine and the pain isn't a problem anymore. Am I upset that the patient is comfortable? Of course not. But I know I'll have to wait until the morphine wears off before I can see if the pain is a clue to a serious underlying illness.

I'm not saying that our pain should prompt us into inspection of our inner life, looking for sin that has caused our suffering. For the majority of illnesses I've seen, there isn't a direct correlation between personal sin and personal physical illness. Suggesting that patients have brought on their own condition only adds to their misery.

But that's not to say that pain doesn't come to us without a purpose. God is interested in conforming us to the image of Christ (Romans 8:29), in testing the mettle of our faith and strengthening our commitments to him in times of ease and in times of disease.

We feel pain. What should we do? Cry out for grace. We want deliverance, but we haven't understood his higher ways. We don't need grace to deal with the pain. In fact, sometimes the pain *is* his grace.

Sometimes grace comes dressed in a cloak of suffering.

I cannot begin to adequately deal with this subject here, but I would suggest looking more deeply at several books, including C. S. Lewis's *The Problem of Pain* and *Pain: The Gift Nobody Wants* by Philip Yancey and Paul Brand. Dr. Brand, a missionary surgeon, assisted thousands of patients with leprosy, a disease that attacks the nerves and leaves people in the self-destructive state of not being able to experience pain. Brand says that the most wonderful gift he could give his patients was the gift of pain.

One of the insidious lies of the prosperity gospel is that it focuses our attention off the Giver and onto the gifts, off of Christ, the treasure of the ages, and onto me as the recipient of material treasures.

God has promised riches to those who love him, but these riches can't be measured by our accountants on tax day. Listen to James:

> Listen, my beloved brothers, has not God chosen those who are poor in the world to be rich in faith and heirs of the kingdom, which he has promised to those who love him?
>
> —James 2:5

Whether he enables us with earthly riches or tests us with poverty, God's posture toward us is always the same: grace. Whether he blesses us with health or allows a path of pain, his love toward his children is unchanging. It is because of his grace that he does not choose for us a path of ease but a path that leads to holiness.

> For the grace of God has appeared, bringing salvation for all people, training us to renounce ungodliness and worldly passions, and to live self-controlled, upright, and godly lives in the present age, waiting for our blessed hope, the appearing of the glory of our great God and Savior Jesus Christ.
>
> —Titus 2:11-13

> For the moment all discipline seems painful rather than pleasant, but later it yields the peaceful fruit of righteousness to those who have been trained by it.
>
> —Hebrews 12:11

We love to sing "Amazing Grace," but there are other adjectives we could use. Training grace. Disciplining grace. But these are the descriptions that are ignored in the masquerade.

We want happiness. God wants holiness.

We want to be pain-free. God wants our trust.

We want riches. He offers a path to eternal blessing.

We want answers. God has questions for us.

We ask for grace. God answers, but sometimes the grace he sends is named "pain."

Have you ever had to deliver a bad-news message and the recipient became angry toward you? Perhaps you reacted like so many others. "Hey, don't shoot me! I'm only the messenger!" Pain is the messenger drawing us closer to the heart of a gracious God.

Let me add a caveat for those of you who deal with patients, friends, or family who are suffering. Because pain is experienced emotionally and not intellectually, a scholarly recitation of God's purpose for pain in the other person's life is unlikely to be received with grace! Please don't default to a callous recitation of Romans 8:28, even though that verse is true. We need to follow Christ's example here. Remember, he is a God who joined us in suffering. It is no mistake that the central focus of our boast as Christians is a man hanging on a cross, racked with suffering for us.

"Why?" isn't the best question.

There are reasons for physical and emotional pain and reasons for financial struggles in the life of the Christian. But it is often easier to say what such pain doesn't mean than to say what it does. It doesn't mean you don't have enough faith. It doesn't mean God is punishing you for your sin.

Searching for answers to the why questions may add to rather than subtract from our misery. In the end, I believe God wants us to press on in spite of not knowing the answers. God is more interested in us having faith without answers than in providing answers to our every question. Faith expressed only in the light is not faith at all.

Just ask my parents, Harry and Mildred Kraus.

It was the summer of 1957, the year my father opened his medical practice in rural Virginia. Life wasn't easy in those days. Besides the rigors of medical education and the financial strain that created, my mother suffered from secondary infertility. What's that? It's the inability to have children after successful pregnancy in the past. After having two sons, my mother had four miscarriages in a row. The obstetrics experts told her she would be unable to have children again. She was disappointed but pressed on because life was busy and full with seven- and nine-year-old sons.

The phone was ringing when my father approached the office door. In those days, struggling to get the practice going, my father always rushed to unlock the door to answer the phone. He could hear the anxiety in the voice of a neighbor. "You'd better come down to the water."

"What's wrong?"

There was no explanation, only a second urging. "We need you to get down here."

My father headed for the James River, not knowing what was in store. He knew that his two sons had wanted to go swimming. Was someone hurt or injured and needed his expertise?

At the river's edge, he found a gathering crowd and my mother, but no sons. The two boys who had brought so much joy had both been swallowed by the James River. The life they knew as a family was shredded in one fateful trip to the river. Never would they hear the jokes of the boys at the dinner table. Never again would my mother be able to quiet her disappointment over her infertility with the thought, *At least I have my two sons.*

At such times we ask, "Why?"

We cry in our pain, demanding answers, but God closes the heavens. We believe answers exist, but for much of our suffering, God's answers seem hidden, his love remote.

Trust only on sunny days is not trust.

Faith moves forward at midnight when the sun is hidden from view.

We search the book of Job, looking for the answers for our pain. How could God in his love have allowed such catastrophe and suffering?

Searching with Job, we long for an answer to the why question. *Why am I suffering?* But the answer never comes, at least not the answer we want. Not even when God speaks from the whirlwind. Look at God's answer, and count the number of questions God asks Job (Job 38–41). I did and lost count after sixty.

The bottom line? God is God—I am not. He wants my trust in the midst of my pain. He gets to be the one to ask the questions, not me.

He does not promise relief. Instead he gives us his presence.

He does not often answer why questions. Instead he asks us, "Who is God?"

God wants to deepen, stretch, and strengthen our faith. Unfortunately for us, deepening involves exposure to dredging tools, stretching involves tension, and strengthening means painful exercise.

"Why?" is a question without a definitive answer for my parents or anyone else experiencing catastrophic loss. We can gather explanations into a blanket around us, but ultimately we will find comforting warmth only in a faith that says, "I will trust without knowing." For people like my parents, answers to why questions offer some comfort, but in the end there are no good explanations for the death of a child. The only real comfort comes with releasing the need to know. We find comfort only when knowing that God knows is enough.

A theology that masquerades as a gospel of grace but doesn't deal with the difficulty of suffering isn't only inadequate—it's dangerous. Proponents of prosperity doctrine build unsteady scaffolding around gullible believers. The scaffolding collapses when the winds of adversity rise. When pain occurs, those taken in by this teaching are left feeling guilty and wondering where their faith has failed. They question God's love, not understanding that God's love was hidden in the pain.

The journey to the promised land doesn't promise deliverance from bondage now, and neither should our theology.

The deception inherent in the masquerade exists because it's what we want to believe. We cling sincerely to teaching that promises health and riches. We would like to believe that the story of the Exodus ends with the celebration on the shore of the Red Sea. *We're out of bondage!* But that's only chapter 15 of Exodus. There was a lot of desert travel and travail ahead: trials, suffering, longing for the good old days, and forty years of wilderness.

Mountain climbers discipline their bodies with vigorous exercise in preparation for reaching the earth's highest peaks. After months of training, they make their ascent in stages, stopping now and then to acclimate to the thin air with its reduced oxygen.

Times of suffering are tantamount to spiritual mountain climbing. We need to prepare for these times with the spiritual disciplines of prayer, Bible study, and time spent in solitude with the Savior.

Carbon monoxide binds so tightly to hemoglobin that no oxygen can be carried. The treatment is oxygen in high concentrations to allow the oxygen to successfully compete with the carbon monoxide for hemoglobin binding sites. So also high concentrations of grace and the true gospel are needed to displace the false prosperity gospel in our lives.

Remember, God's grace does not always appear as soft, rose-petaled comfort. Sometimes grace touches us with a loving hand of pain.

When Christ's hand reaches out to guide us through a valley of pain, look carefully at the hands that are holding ours. His hands are scarred, etched with evidence of pain. Precious. Amazing. The hands of the Creator of the universe carry the wounds of love for his children.

They are the scars of grace.

For further Reflection

1. How is the prosperity gospel like carbon monoxide? How does it masquerade as gospel truth?

2. "A belief system that lacks a theology of suffering is not only errant, it is damaging to the human soul afflicted with pain." Do you agree or disagree?

3. How can pain be a good thing? If pain is God's messenger, what is the message? What does God want to accomplish through your suffering?

4. How does God's grace relate to your pain? You may want happiness and riches and no pain. What does God want for you?

5. Instead of asking God, "Why?" what would be a better question to ask him? Instead of giving you relief or the cessation of suffering, what does God want to give you?

PART THREE

Treating Gospel Debt

CHAPTER FIFTEEN

Defining Oxygen, Defining Grace

've been the personal beneficiary of liberal amounts of oxygen in the atmosphere since the moment I took my first breath. And for the vast majority of that time I had no idea that I needed it. In fact, other than in chemistry classes or in my medical education where I tried to understand oxygen delivery and consumption, I didn't give oxygen even a passing thought. Unaware, we breathe, taking it in, life in an invisible molecule.

The only time most of us even give oxygen a passing thought is when we're in oxygen debt and even then automatic brain functions kick in, driving us to breathe more quickly and making our hearts beat faster. More oxygen is delivered to our needy tissues without our conscious recognition. The only thing we're conscious of is an urgency to get more air.

Every time a surgeon fixes an abdominal aortic aneurysm, the same urgency is felt. The aorta is the big blood vessel that exits the heart carrying all of the blood that is dispersed to the body. An aneurysm is a ballooning up of a section of an artery, creating a weak area prone to rupture. It can be thought of as a bubble. The bigger the bubble, the more likely it is to bust.

An aortic aneurysm is an aneurysm of the largest blood vessel in the body. In order to fix it, the surgeon needs to stop the blood flow through the aorta. This is done by applying a delicate clamp across the blood vessel above and below the bubble. Of course, this intentionally places all of the tissues served by the area below the clamps into oxygen debt. Because all of the body needs a continuous supply of oxygen to live, the surgery must be done swiftly and efficiently. When the clamp is placed, the surgeon calls out, "Aortic clamp on." Likewise, as soon as the clamp is removed, the surgeon reports, "Aortic clamp off." As soon as I've done this, I want to know, "What was the cross-clamp time?" I want to know how long the tissues were starved of oxygen. Few other operations create this kind of urgency in my mind.

I do all of this without really thinking about oxygen. Of course, I know that's why I feel an inward urge to push forward when the aortic cross-clamp is on, but I really don't think of oxygen in such a way that I could define it.

Ask anyone around you to define oxygen, and you'll likely see a blank expression.

"It's the air."

Not really, but there's oxygen in the air.

"It's invisible."

True, but that doesn't define it, does it?

"It's the stuff we breathe so we can survive."

True again, and a bit closer to a functional understanding, but we still haven't landed on a definition.

If you've taken high-school chemistry, perhaps your definition would include an understanding of the molecular weight of an oxygen atom and how the oxygen we breathe is actually a molecule of two oxygen atoms joined by a mysterious chemical force.

My point? Just that something so important to us often goes undefined, unrecognized, and unappreciated.

Until we're faced with a few seconds without it.

Grace is a bit that way. It is equally important, but most of us have only a vague notion as to what it really is. I've spent this entire book talking about it but haven't directly defined it since the Introduction because I wanted to give you a picture of how grace functions in order to lay a foundation for our understanding. Similarly, defining the molecular makeup of oxygen is less important to a physician than knowing how to deal with causes of airway obstruction, emphysema, embolus, and sepsis.

We've looked at the things that block the flow of grace in our lives and the things we can do to open the graceway so we can learn to stand firm in the grace of God. We have a saying on the foreign mission field: Vision is better caught than taught. That simply means there is nothing like direct exposure to teach a person what it is like to carry out the Great Commission on the mission field. You can listen to lectures or read a book, but there's nothing quite like doing something in order to really understand it.

Grace is that way. I wanted to give you an idea of how grace functions and what kind of things can interrupt the grace in our lives before expanding our biblical definition. In the end you can read these words, but if you aren't experiencing grace, true understanding is going to remain elusive; a concept on paper can never define grace outside of experience.

Remember the definition I gave in the Introduction?

**Grace is a godly characteristic that determines God's posture
toward his children whereby he generously and freely loves,
forgives, favors, and exalts undeserving sinners into sonship.**

Let's break it down. Grace is *a godly characteristic*. The kind of grace
I'm talking about cannot be defined outside of God himself. Jesus is
the ultimate manifestation of God's grace.

> And the Word became flesh and dwelt among us, and
> we have seen his glory, glory as of the only Son from the
> Father, full of grace and truth. . . . And from his fullness
> we have all received, grace upon grace. For the law was
> given through Moses; grace and truth came through Jesus
> Christ.
>
> —John 1:14, 16-17

Yes, humans can have grace, but the quality is a divine one. We are
merely stewards of God's grace.

It is a characteristic that *determines God's posture toward his children*. His posture toward us is love. It doesn't take grace to love the
lovely. But he loved us in our sinful state. That's where grace comes
in. Grace is the quality that allows God to show love to undeserving sinners.

A chief characteristic of grace is the fact that it is given as a free
gift. Generously. Favor shown to a student who made all A's on a
report card is not grace. Inherent in the definition of grace is that it
is freely given to the undeserving. That's what makes it grace and not
wages. In the New Testament the word often translated "gift" comes
from the root Greek word for *grace*. The fact that grace is a gift is a
defining quality.

The dominant New Testament context for demonstrating God's
grace is salvation. So that's how grace is commonly defined. Because
of his grace, he showers his love and forgiveness on undeserving
sinners.

But grace isn't a minor characteristic that God showed toward us once by putting our names on some divine roll book and then laying it aside. His grace remains the consistent, unmoving quality that determines his every action toward his children.

Some people think of grace as weakness, as an antithesis to justice. Don't misunderstand. God's grace may include motherly kindness, but it is not to be misrepresented as anything frail. God's grace to us came at an extreme cost to himself, the death of his only Son as a sacrifice for our sins. Perhaps you've heard of "cheap grace," a phrase first coined by the theologian/pastor Dietrich Bonhoeffer,[19] which conveys the attitude that grace is free, so why not sin? A person who treats the grace of God with such contempt is in a sad state of ignorance. God's grace is free but far from cheap. *Cheap* is finding God's favor by performance. *Priceless* is receiving his love at the cost of the cross.

Have you ever heard the term *greasy grace*? It refers to treating God with presumption. *God is a God of grace. So I'll just sin, ask forgiveness, and everything will be OK.* God's grace is costly and precious. To such an attitude, Paul replied with a resounding, "By no means!" (Romans 6:2; KJV, "God forbid").

We often mistakenly think of grace as a peripheral characteristic of God, an ornamental attribute like kindness or goodness. But grace is at the center of God's character. It is as if grace is the operating system that guides our every interaction with our Father. Just as the Microsoft Windows program in some way frames almost all of your interaction with your computer's hard drive, so grace frames God's interactions with his children. Every action toward us is accomplished through his grace.

Likewise every gift, every talent, and even every breath is evidence of his grace. And because grace is a gift to the undeserving, guess who gets the credit? God.

The Bible teaches that we are "stewards of God's . . . grace" (1 Peter 4:10). Just as it frames his every action and his posture toward us, so I believe grace should take its rightful place in the center of our posture

toward a hurting world. In 2 Corinthians, Paul encouraged the believers
to be generous toward others and called this an "act of grace."

> But as you excel in everything—in faith, in speech, in
> knowledge, in all earnestness, and in our love for you—see
> that you excel in this act of grace also.
>
> —8:7

Paul realized that whatever work was accomplished through his
hands was an evidence of God's grace.

> But by the grace of God I am what I am, and his grace
> toward me was not in vain. On the contrary, I worked
> harder than any of them, though it was not I, but the
> grace of God that is with me.
>
> —1 Corinthians 15:10

We are whatever we are because of God's grace. Our every accomplishment, from the mundane to the spectacular, is a witness to his
grace. And to that end God is the one who gets the glory.

> For it is all for your sake, so that as grace extends to more
> and more people it may increase thanksgiving, to the glory
> of God.
>
> —2 Corinthians 4:15

In the New Testament we see descriptions of being taught by grace,
being "under grace," and standing in grace. Peter said it this way as he
concluded his first letter:

> I have written briefly to you, exhorting and declaring that
> this is the true grace of God. Stand firm in it.
>
> —1 Peter 5:12

I described the urgency I feel to efficiently move through aortic
aneurysm surgery because the lower half of the patient's body is in

oxygen debt. Why don't we feel a similar urgency to shower grace on ourselves and others when gospel debt is present?

Too many members of the western church have misunderstood the centrality of grace to the Christian walk. Perhaps they walked a church aisle and made a public confession of their faith, but they seem to have left God's grace at the altar! Of course, that's impossible, but in their understanding of their ongoing need for grace, that's effectively what they've done.

We need grace every day. Every moment. Continuous exposure to oxygen is essential for life. Continuous exposure to grace is essential for spiritual life.

And now that Christ is not present in bodily form, walking the hills of Galilee, we are the chief conduits of his presence to a dying world.

We are the chief conduits of grace to a dying world.

Grace cannot be peripheral. It is the single most important characteristic that will set us apart from every graceless, works-oriented religious follower. Grace can no longer be seen as ornamental embellishments (remember grace notes?) but as the major chord that undergirds every melody of our lives. We were saved by grace. Now we live by grace, work by grace, and play by grace. Grace is manifested in every good deed and in every kind word and in every right action.

But grace is not only seen in kindness. God's grace toward us is manifest both in his gentleness and in his harsh rebuke. We see it in our health and in our suffering. Because we understand his character, we receive all things as gifts from his hand, manifestations of his grace, whether they bring happiness or sorrow. Because grace frames his posture toward me, even in times of pain I can believe that my experience is a manifestation of his grace.

How can we walk in grace saturation, breathing in and breathing out his grace in a constant cycle?

Realize that you need grace continuously. *A* is for *acknowledge your need*. Not just once at salvation. Not just daily. Continuously! Just like oxygen. Staying in grace takes moment-by-moment recognition of our need.

Choose to stand firm in grace. That means choosing to believe the gospel promises. Standing implies a stationary posture. We don't receive grace one time and move on. We *stay* in grace. The gospel of grace means it's his work by his grace through us and he gets the glory. That relieves us of the need to worry. *B* is for *believing the gospel*. Continuously.

Step C naturally follows. When we realize our continuous need and look to Christ for the solution (*A* and *B*), we will begin to commune with Christ. *C* is for *communion*, the step in which we see the penetration of the gospel of grace into every area of our lives.

Practicing grace recognition every moment produces humility and gratefulness and promotes good grace stewardship.

After every good thing that comes our way, we should think, *That's God's grace*. When you open your eyes in the morning, you've been given the gift of life for another day. Think, *That's God's grace to me*. If you can enjoy a meal today, think, *That's grace*. If you ride in an automobile, think, *This is God's grace*. If you have to walk instead, thank God for your ability to do so and think, *This is God's grace*. Every breath we take is evidence of his grace.

Do you have sight? That's grace. Can you smell a flower? Grace again. Have you ever appreciated a comfy sofa, a favorite chair, a cold soda, or the laughter of a child? All grace. Virtually every minute, God's grace is touching you.

Do you realize that you can change your feelings by changing your thinking? Training your mind to receive everything in your life as evidence of God's grace does something to you: you feel thankful.

As you begin to recognize the pervasiveness of God's grace in your life, remember that inherent in the definition of grace is that we don't deserve it. It is *unmerited.* That's why it's grace. Keeping that part of the definition in constant focus keeps us firmly in the practice of humility, the very thing that keeps the graceway open!

Take a breath and realize that you didn't deserve it. Every moment is a gift. And every moment we can function as a steward of that gift.

So go ahead. Breathe in. That's God's grace.

Now exhale grace on a dying world.

For Further Reflection

1. What is the definition of grace? How does it function or work in our lives?

2. What does it mean that we are "stewards" of God's grace? For what purpose?

3. What is the connection between the words *grace* and *gift*? What does the element of being undeserved have to do with grace?

4. Why are some people mistaken to think of divine grace as weakness? How is God's grace seen in both his acceptance and his rebuke?

5. Does God truly see you as a conduit of his grace to a dying world? How so? Do you see this as a burden or a privilege? How can non-Christians around you see God's grace in your life?

CHAPTER SIXTEEN

The Danger of Noncompliance

We physicians have a term for patients who can't or won't follow our instructions: noncompliant.

It's not a very complimentary term. It conveys the idea that the patient is responsible for a treatment failure. The patient didn't improve? It wasn't the doctor's fault. The patient didn't take the medicines as prescribed. The patient was noncompliant.

One of the areas where this can pose particular difficulties is in the area of antibiotic treatment for infection. A physician prescribes a medicine regimen, let's say a pill to be taken three times a day for ten days. So the patient begins the therapy, happy to comply because he or she feels so miserable.

After three or four days, the patient's fever has disappeared, and other symptoms such as a sore throat begin to abate. So now the medicine doesn't seem so necessary. Taking medicine when you feel healthy seems stupid. The first day a person feels well they miss one dose out of the three. The next day they look at the bottle and think, *This is crazy. I'm not sick anymore. I'm going to save this until I need it again someday.* So the patient shoves the medicine into the back of the cabinet.

The problem lies in the deviousness of certain types of bacteria that attack us. Once exposed to the chemical assault of antibiotics, the bacteria begin to die—not all of them, but a predictable percentage with each new wave of antibiotic. The bacteria that have not yet been killed focus quickly on devising a new survival strategy. They mutate and acquire new talents to resist the medication. If the waves of medication assault cease at this point, the surviving mutated bacteria multiply, resilient and stronger. At this point, the patient feels worse again and digs into the back of the medicine cabinet for the lonely pills. But now it's too late. The bacteria are smarter now, and when they see the chemical assault coming, they are resistant and refuse to die. If the patient returns to the physician, a new medication will have to be prescribed, something newer, stronger, and undoubtedly more expensive.

The physician will sigh and write a note in the patient record: "Noncompliant."

We can attribute a portion of the responsibility for this problem to our instant culture. In the developed world we have grown impatient and demanding. We are microwave-savvy, but marinade-challenged. We like our banking to be drive-through, our grocery lines to be ten items or fewer, and our oil changes to be in a "jiffy." We like fast food, broadband, interstate travel, and news headlines every thirty minutes.

The old and slow are pushed aside to make room for the newer and faster. We are a people who buy next year's models in October and purchase our tans in spray-applications. Express mail. Bullet trains. High-speed Internet. Instant access. Rapid results.

Out with the old. In with the new.

We want our cures to be quick and our dosing to be once daily.

Inherent to many cultures in the developing world are constant reminders to slow down. The absence of the latest modern conveniences has helped create a culture where relationships, not schedules, take first priority. When I was preparing this chapter, I hiked up into the mountains near our home along the edge of the Great Rift Valley. As I walked up a path through the forest, thorns from a "wait-a-bit bush" grabbed my clothing as I passed. I paused to disentangle myself, smiling at the thought that even the plant life in Africa seems to speak the same message: "Slow down."

It's dangerous to let our instant culture carry over into our spiritual life. That remains my biggest concern in presenting an ABC format for the treatment of gospel debt. The ABC plan doesn't imply an instant cure—three easy steps to Christian maturity and grace saturation. But that's what we long for. *Please God, let's just get over the trials. I want patience. Now.*

But God heads up what some have called "The Department of Redundancy Department." That means he lets us relearn life lessons over and over and over again as he patiently forms us into the image of his Son. However, when it comes to following God's prescription for staying out of gospel debt, we are mired in the mud of noncompliance.

In physical resuscitation, our concern for airway, breathing, and circulation is ongoing. Within seconds of a problem in any of these areas, a patient can fall into oxygen debt.

Our physical life, however robust, is surprisingly fragile. At any moment in time we balance on a razor edge only seconds away from life-threatening oxygen debt.

A problem with airway, breathing, or circulation can occur with alarming suddenness. Cut off oxygen and within seconds, life is under siege, threatened with the precipice of death. Most of us never think this way. Our Creator has made us in such a way as to make continuous intake of oxygen an automatic function. Built-in checks and balances are all a part of an ingenious design. The trachea is twice as big as needed to meet the oxygen demands under normal circumstances. We know this because cancers of the voice box can narrow the trachea by one half before the patient has any problem breathing at all.

Similarly and sadly, at any moment in time we live only seconds away from gospel debt. It saddens and amazes me how quickly I can turn from rejoicing in the adequacy of the cross to judging my brother, sinful anger, anxiety, or a myriad of other symptoms pointing to gospel debt and my need for grace.

That's why I want to caution against viewing the spiritual ABC approach as a one-time quick fix. I've assembled the ABC's as a tool to help jog our memories, not as a three-step, effortless launch into spiritual maturity. More than anything, my hope is that my treatment guidelines will nudge us toward a life of grace appreciation, a life where grace recognition is constant and grace exhalation is the natural result. The foundation of such a life is repentance, faith, and communion that cycle as regularly as breathing.

Yes, we all fight the tendency to engage in spiritual noncompliance. We want to follow the ABC's one time, feel better, and shove the recommendations into the back of the medicine cabinet.

Breathing grace, the inflow and outflow of Christ's gospel into a breathless world, is by design a continuous process. Recognition of our need and reliance on his promises are keys to healthy spiritual respiration and thus a vibrant and fulfilled life.

In the hospital I often write orders for patients who require higher concentrations of oxygen. I write the concentration as well as the route—i.e., O_2 2 liters/minute via nasal cannula, or perhaps 40% O_2 via face mask. I imagine that God has written a similar prescription order for us and sends us to a pharmacy that has an unlimited, free supply:

100% grace via continuous inhalation

God's grace. So amazing. Available in unlimited supply to undeserving sinners like me. He has opened heaven's pharmacy. The invitation is ours. Let it not be written in our heavenly charts: "Noncompliant with needed therapy."

For Further Reflection

1. "The ABC plan doesn't imply an instant cure—three easy steps to Christian maturity." Do you find this disappointing or encouraging? Why? Is there an instant cure to our spiritual faults?

2. Why does God let you learn the same lessons over and over? What does this show you about him? About ourselves?

3. Why do you so quickly revert to gospel debt and a grace shortage? Does this give you good reason to give up? Why or why not?

4. What do you think of God's prescription for our souls: "100% grace via continuous inhalation"? Explain.

5. What spiritual lesson has made the greatest impact on you during these studies? Why? How will you follow up on all that you have learned so that it remains part of your life for the long term?

Notes

1. For more on how we use the word *grace*, see Philip Yancey, *What's So Amazing About Grace?* (Grand Rapids, MI: Zondervan, 1997), pp. 12–13 and Brennan Manning, *The Ragamuffin Gospel* (Sisters, OR: Multnomah, 1990), pp. 16–17.

2. Ibid.

3. Joseph Hart, "Come, Ye Sinners, Poor and Wretched," 1759.

4. For a full understanding of the chart that I've described, see *Gospel Transformation* (Jenkintown, PA: World Harvest Mission, 2001, 2002), pp. 107–111 and the diagram in the back of the book entitled "The Cross Chart," copyright 2001 by World Harvest Mission.

5. John Piper, *Future Grace* (Sisters, OR: Multnomah, 1998, 2005).

6. *Gospel Transformation*, p. 91.

7. Ibid.

8. Ibid.

9. For a more complete discussion of the disciplines of silence and solitude, see Charles R. Swindoll, *Intimacy with the Almighty* (Dallas: Word, 1996).

10. See Henri J. M. Nouwen, *The Way of the Heart* (New York: Ballantine, 1983, 2003), p. 15.

11. Ibid., p. 21.

12. Ibid.

13. John Piper, *Don't Waste Your Life* (Wheaton, IL: Crossway Books, 2003), p. 108.

14. Ibid., p. 109.

15. Nouwen, *The Way of the Heart*. p. 21.

16. Stan Guthrie, "A Crescent or a Cross: Islam Prospers in America," *Christianity Today*, October 28, 1991, p. 40.

17. *Gospel Transformation*, p. 35.

18. C. S. Lewis, *The Four Loves* (Eugene, OR: Harvest House, 1971), pp. 111–112.

19. Dietrich Bonhoeffer, *The Cost of Discipleship* (London: SCM Press Ltd., 1948), p. 35.

Scripture Index

Genesis

2:7   43

Exodus

15   148

Leviticus

19:18   108

1 Samuel

16:7   118

2 Samuel

24   76

1 Chronicles

21   76

2 Chronicles

7:14   45

Job

38–41   147

Psalms

1:2-3   67

119:11   86

Proverbs

22:17   127

28:13   45

Isaiah

28:9-10   66

Jeremiah

2:13   44

Hosea

10:12   127

Zechariah

4:6-7   138

Matthew

6:25-26, 34   56
13:22   129
18:3   45
23:24-28   114

Mark

8:36-38   107

Luke

6:41-42   86
9:23   85

John

1:14, 16-17   156
3:16   52
14:1   129
15:4-5   67

Romans

5:1   52
5:1-2   33
5:2   15, 52
6:2   157
6:14   14
6:22-23   31
8:1   32
8:28   146
8:29   144

1 Corinthians

15:10   158
15:31   85

2 Corinthians

2:14-15   106
3:18   87
4:15   158
8:7   158
12:9   13

Galatians

1:6-9   121
3:3   119
3:14   32
5:1   120

Ephesians

1:3-4   32
2:7   14
2:8-9   52
3:8   32

Philippians

4:6-7   129
4:19   31

Colossians

2:6   53
2:7   53

1 Thessalonians

5:16-18   75

Titus

2:11-12   88
2:11-13   145

Hebrews

4:7   94

4:15-16	75	**1 Peter**	
10:12-13	117	3:15	107
10:24-25	97	4:10	14, 157
11:1	54	5:12	158
11:6	54		
12:11	145	**2 Peter**	
12:15	136	3:18	14, 63
13:15	74		
		1 John	
James		1: 6	116
1:22-24	95	1:6-9	116
2:5	144	1:7	117
2:18	54	1:8	117
4:6	45	1:9	116, 117